History of Headley

Headley Heath, Bellamoss Pond./ *Courtesy, K Scowen F.R.P.S.*

HISTORY OF
HEADLEY

edited by
J. C. Stuttard

LEATHERHEAD AND DISTRICT
LOCAL HISTORY SOCIETY

2001

'History is a pattern of timeless moments'

T. S. Eliot (from 'Little Gidding')

ISBN 0 9506009 9 7

Front cover photograph by Gwen Hoad
Church of St Mary the Virgin, Headley

Printed by J.W. Arrowsmith Ltd, Bristol

FOREWORD

This book on Headley is published by the Leatherhead and District Local History Society, in style and content similar to those already produced on Fetcham, Ashtead and Leatherhead. To provide histories of this kind has long been one of the principal aims of the Society.

A large part of the task of assembling this book has been undertaken by Jack Stuttard who not only wrote several of its chapters but also edited the whole work. Other members of the Society and local Headley residents who helped in the writing and the research are referred to in the Preface.

The prime aim of the book is to interest readers in the history of Headley, so that they can take away a picture of the village today and what it was like in past centuries. Comments would be welcomed by the Society.

Peter Tarplee
Chairman

Leatherhead and District Local History Society
64 Church Street
Leatherhead
KT22 8DP

PREFACE

There have been a number of short accounts of Headley but this is the first book giving details of the village's history from pre-Roman times to the present day. Although all the main periods of English history are covered, the 19th and 20th centuries are concentrated on with a glance at the Millennium Year 2000 and beyond.

The production of a book of this kind depends on the co-operation and help of many, not least the Society's Chairman, Peter Tarplee, who co-ordinated the work involved and wrote the Foreword. Contributors included Richard Butler, Ernest Crossland, Peter Denyer, Hugh Fortescue, Alan Gillies and Brian Godfrey. They not only wrote for the book but also helped in the selection of its illustrations.

Source materials for the book were obtained from the Surrey History Centre in Woking and the Public Record Office at Kew; the British Library and the Minet Library in London were also consulted. We are grateful to all these for their advice and help. Access to the parish records was kindly made available by the Rector of Headley, the Rev David Wotton. Particular thanks are due to the Domestic Buildings Research Group (Surrey) which allowed the Society to use its valuable reports on Headley's old buildings. Sophie Chessum of the National Trust Office at Polesden Lacey contributed a great deal of material on Headley Heath and its history. Julie Lawrence of the Surrey Wildlife Trust gave us all that was needed on Nower Wood. Some old inventories, made by people in the village, were obtained from Marion Herridge, their transcriber. The Hon. Robert Bridges' advice on Headley matters was particularly appreciated. Kenneth Clew was always most helpful on source material. An account by Tim Richardson of the Canadian Forces at Headley in wartime was especially valued, as was the help offered by the Defence Services Medical Rehabilitation Centre at Headley Court. Fl. Lt. Neil

Williams R.A.F. gave us much on this, including photographs. Information on Headley Cricket Club was generously provided by Sir Michael and Lady Pickard. Tyrells Wood Golf Club presented the Society with a copy of their latest booklet on its history.

The Society's Library and its *Proceedings* were valuable sources on Headley, as were the Leatherhead Public Library and the publications of the Surrey Archaeological Society. Census information is reproduced with the permission of the Controller of Her Majesty's Stationery Office, ©, Crown Copyright.

J.C. Stuttard   2001.

CONTENTS

LIST OF ILLUSTRATIONS

Frontispiece: Headley Heath

Unless otherwise stated, all the illustrations are taken from the Society Collection or from the P. Denyer Collection.

Chapter 1

INTRODUCTION

Headley is a small Downland village between Mickleham on the west and Walton-on-the-Hill on the east, also only a few miles from Leatherhead, Ashtead and Epsom. Brockham, Betchworth and Dorking are not far away to the south. The village has a high and commanding position on the North Downs and through the centuries until the present time it has maintained its rural individuality helped by an attractive mix of rolling grass slopes, heath and woodland. The spire of St Mary's Parish Church is an impressive landmark and on a fine day the view from the church covers a wide spectrum of the Surrey countryside.

The North Downs at Headley reach a height of 187m (c. 613ft) not far from Oyster Hill and Tot Hill, much of Headley Heath being about the same above sea level though there is a steep fall on the western side. The lowest point of the Headley parish is a little under 100m (c. 328ft) along the Lodge Bottom Road near Warren Farm. The parish is about two miles from north to south, tapering rather at both extremes. The narrow point of the boundary in the north is crossed by a short stretch of the M25 motorway, with underpasses along Tilley Lane and Hurst Lane. The parish is broadest at the central point of it, extending for about a mile and a half from Headley village to the Tyrells Wood Golf Course. The southern parish boundary diverts to take in part of the Box Hill Road becoming the eastern part of the parish boundary after this.

The village has been called 'Headley' for a long time but in medieval years there were many forms of its spelling. In the Domesday Book of 1086 it is called 'Hallega' and in documents of 12th–14th centuries it appears as 'Hadlega', 'Hetlega' and 'Hetherlegh'. It seems to have carried its present form first in Queen Elizabeth I's reign, though there were small fluctuations in more recent times, The spelling of 'Headley' was officially adopted by the Parish Council in 1899. The name means 'Heath clearing' or 'Clearing overgrown with heather'.[1]

Geology and Soils

Much of Headley lies on a sub-stratum of chalk which is part of the northern limb of an anticlinal structure known as the Weald. In fact the chalk dips away northwards from Headley to pass beneath the outcrops of the younger Eocene sands and clay forming the London Basin. The boundary between the chalk and the Eocene runs from the south-west to north-east about two miles to the north of the village. Between these sands and clays and Headley itself the land surface apart from soil is entirely chalk but south of Headley much of the chalk is covered by a veneer of superficial material. The one exception is the Nower Wood area which is an isolated site of Eocene strata completely detached from the main area to the north. The superficial material is largely mapped by the Geological Survey as Clay-with-Flints.[2]

The last geological survey of the district took place from 1928 to 1930. Since then research by other workers has shown that some of the areas mapped as being covered by Clay-with-Flints are not so. However, sands and gravels of supposedly Pliocene age are mentioned.

The chalk at Headley is a pure white limestone laid down in a warm sea during the late Cretaceous period which ended about 70 million years age. One of its main features are the bands of flints. Flints are put to good use in buildings as, for example, in the walls of Headley Church. Following the end of the Cretaceous period there must have been a long spell of erosion as we know the layers of the chalk have been removed, so the junction with the overlying Eocene deposits is an unconformable one.

The Eocene period deposits occur in Nower Wood. The junction with the chalk is marked by the Bullhead Bed which is a thin layer of dark clay and greenish sand. The bed is followed by about two metres of Thanet Sands, a marine deposit laid down by a sea which eventually extended its influence to lay down the Woolwich/Reading Beds; at Nower Wood they are regarded as being of the Woolwich facies. At Oyster Hill, where these Woolwich facies were

Fig. 1. View from Church Lane, looking towards Tumber Street

Fig. 2. Tumber Street, from Leech Lane

exposed, specimens of the fossil oyster, *Ostrea Bellovacina*, have been obtained from time to time. This is a typical fossil from these beds.

Following the deposition of the Woolwich-Reading Beds there was a long period during which any later Eocene deposits such as the London Clay, if deposited, would have been removed by erosion. There was a final marine invasion which took place during the late Pliocene or early Pleistocene period and is known as the Calabrian Sea. The effect of this sea can be studied by examining a north-south longitudinal section through the Headley area. There was a distinct bevelling in the chalk surface almost to the top of the Downs. When this Pliocene sea retreated it left behind what are known as the Headley Heath deposits. These deposits can be seen capping the Eocene strata at Nower Wood, where they are about two metres thick, and on Headley Heath where in places they form ridges. They consist of moderately well sorted yellow brown coarse sands with isolated ferruginous sandstone masses and abundant, rounded, battered flint pebbles. The lack of fossils in these beds is a big difficulty in correlating then with similar deposits elsewhere. As mentioned earlier, the geological map shows then as Clay-with-Flints but there is one indication that Headley Heath has sands and gravels of doubtful Pliocene age. Clay-with-Flints does occur, as it is quite a common sort of superficial material associated with the chalk. Originally, it was regarded as a residual material left behind from solution effects on the chalk. However, it is now generally accepted that the origin is probably more complex than this.

The Pleistocene period followed the Pliocene about two million years ago and the present topographic features of the Headley district began to take shape . Most of the late Pleistocene years were occupied by what is termed the Ice Age. However, the glaciers which advanced and retreated several times never actually reached Headley. At times of ice advance Headley would have been in the tundra or periglacial area. However, in times of thaw there was a lot more water about than today with the water table in the chalk at a very high level or even at the surface. The local valley systems would have been fashioned, especially the Headley valley, which probably had a stream flowing down it to the River Mole. However, valleys in chalk country only support streams if the water table is at or near the surface so when the water table falls the stream will go underground.

Today the Headley valley, close to the village, is completely dry.

However, it has in places quite steep sides, an unusual feature for a chalk valley once cut out by a stream. It is suggested that when the water table fell below the floor of the valley the stream would have gone down into swallow holes, a feature that can be seen today with the River Mole at Boxhill. In such a case the stream would be directing most of its energy in cutting downwards to reach an elusive water table, thus leaving very little energy for lateral erosion.

There are now no streams in the Headley area. After heavy rain minor streams may form on Headley Heath, one, for example, starts west of Brimmer Pond but it eventually disappears into the chalk. It is fairly safe to assume that the water going into the chalk takes an underground course with a dip to the Eocene boundary to the north where there is a spring line. At Nower Wood the clays of the Eocene strata cause most of the rainfall to run off, some of which finds its way to well-developed swallow holes along the north-east margin of the wood. The only natural spring recorded in the Headley area is at Oyster Hill, the water probably coming out from the Thanet Sands.

Water Supplies

Before the first supply of mains water in 1897 most of Headley residents obtained their water from wells, tanks or rainwater butts. The spring at Oyster Hill was used as a further source or water. Many of the large houses and some of the old cottages had a well of their own.

Most of Headley's water supply today comes from the Headley Reservoir off Box Hill Road and from Betchworth Tower. Boreholes outside the district at Kenley and Smitham also provide the village with water. Some of the ponds were at one time used by farmers.[3]

Conservation Areas

Headley Heath: This important conservation area has been owned by the National Trust since 1946 (see p.62).[4] The Trust has also bought Oyster Hill Wood and Warren Farm. The Heath is part of the Mole Gap to Reigate Site of Special Scientific Interest (SSSI) notified by 'English Nature' under Section 28 of the Wildlife and Countryside Act 1981. In this special mention is made of Headley Heath, especially the acidic plateau deposits which support ling, bell heather and dwarf furze. Mention is also made of what is termed chalk heath where special conditions allow both acid and lime loving plants to grow side by side. Heather and bracken are common in many parts. One of the ponds has a rare protected plant, the star fruit, *Damasonium alisma*.

The Heath covers an area of 482 acres south and west of Headley village. A short walk from the car park opposite the Cricket Ground gives fine views towards the 'Little Switzerland' valley and in the direction of Polesden Lacey, while further away is the prominent

Fig. 3. Headley Heath, Brimmer Pond

landmark of Ranmore Church. Some well-engineered pathways and tracks cross the Heath in several directions, The long and wide Bridges' Track, along Middle Hill and flanked on its sides by woodland, is named after Sir Edward (later Lord) Bridges* who in the early 1950s, with the help of the Territorials, cleared birch and scrub to achieve the path he wanted. Jubilee Track, some way east of this, was completed during the Queen's Silver Jubilee Celebrations in 1977 and five years earlier the nearby Aspen Track was laid by the Royal Engineers, naming it after some aspen trees in the neighbourhood. There are, of course, many other routes which the visitor can take, permitting much of the Heath to be explored. Some of these are quite broad, acting as 'Firebreaks', many introduced following the devastating and extensive fire in 1976. There are a number of bridleways and tracks for horse-riding over some parts of the Heath. Scattered stretches of woodland are found over wide areas, especially on the steep slopes descending to Lodge Bottom Road, though there are plenty of trees to be seen in the south-central parts of the Heath. Oak trees are often found here are well as birch and a few Scots pine; there are several other types of tree on the southern edge of the Heath, including larch, beech, sycamore, hornbeam and yew.

When walking over the Heath ponds are frequently met with, a few like Brimmer and Hopeful being shown on some 19th century maps. The ponds, most of them artificial, are often formed in hollows where the particular soil holds water; all, except Brimmer, usually dry up in summer. The sites of two other ponds, Bellamoss and Aspen, were specially selected where the view round them is reflected in their water.

Nower Wood: This is an ancient piece of woodland close to Slough Lane and Oyster Hill in the north of Headley village. Nower Wood was purchased in 1971 as an educational reserve by the Surrey Wildlife Trust and has been registered with Surrey County Planning Office as a Regionally Important Geological Site.[5]

Nower Wood has many different rocks and soils, an excellent example of an outlier showing an exposure of Headley Heath gravels; on the northern edge there are some swallows or sink holes. There

---

* Sir Edward (later Lord) Bridges was Chairman of Headley Heath Committee from its formation in 1946 until his death in 1969. He had been at one time Secretary to Churchill's Wartime Cabinet and later Head of the Civil Service. Humphrey Mackworth Praed and Robert Hunter also played an important part in managing the Heath, together with the National Trust.

Fig. 4.   Highland Cattle on the Heath. The cattle are used for conservation grazing

Fig. 5.   A path through Nower Wood. *Courtesy, Surrey Wildlife Trust*

are several pools and some marshland. The trees here are oaks and sweet chestnuts as the main canopy, the understores being holly, silver birch and hazel; on the sandy soil beech is common. Scots pine and larch also grow here. Foxes, badgers, squirrels and deer inhabit the woods which in spring are brightened by bluebells, anemones and primroses. Woodpeckers, nuthatches, blue tits and woodcocks are some of the birds that can be seen.

The Warren: This important part of the chalk downland, close to the Lodge Bottom Road, is protected by the Praedland Estate.

Weather Fluctuations; Freezes, Downpours, Droughts and Storms

Headley has a high position on the Downs and because of this is liable to weather excesses. There was a big freeze to rival that of 1947 in the winter of 1962/63. Snow which fell on the ground in late December 1962 was still there in mid-March 1963 and some blizzards continued to follow after this, accompanied by very low temperatures and cold east winds. Five years later, in 1968, some of the heaviest rains ever recorded occurred and the lower parts of Ashtead and Leatherhead suffered severe flooding. The great drought of 1976 will be equally well remembered when there were unusually high temperatures from mid-June onwards; many fields became brown and everyone was being persuaded to use as little water as possible in their homes. The autumn and winter rains later in the year helped to solve the water problems.

Another unusual weather phenomenon occurred in October 1987 when a particularly violent storm caused a great deal of damage in its path over a wide area, including Headley. There was another gale, similarly destructive, in January 1990, followed a year later by one of the coldest winters and by a summer (in 1991) with particularly high temperatures. The 1995 summer was almost as hot but after a remarkably warm autumn the year ended with heavy snowfalls and dangerous driving conditions, which continued into 1996.

Heavy clouds spoilt the viewing of the solar eclipse on 11th August 1999. There were long spells of rain and strong winds in the later months of the year 2000. the present year opening with biting frosts and occasional snowfalls. The spring and summer months were to prove as varied in the weather as they so often are.

Notes

1. J.E.B. Gover, A. Mawer & E.M. Stenton, *The Place Names of Surrey* (1982)
2. The geological information is based on the following: H.G. Dines & F.H. Edmunds, 'The Geology of the Country around Reigate' HMSO, 1933 (this is printed on the current Geological Map, 286); 'The Geology of Nower Wood' Surrey Wildlife Trust; 'Superficial Deposits of the North Downs' Unpublished paper presented to the British Association Meeting, 1975
3. Hugh Fortescue, *Water Sources in Headley* (1995)
4. Information on Headley Heath was kindly provided by Sophie Chessum of the National Trust at Polesden Lacey
5. Julie Lawrence's help on Nower Wood was much appreciated

Chapter 2

HEADLEY BEFORE THE NORMAN CONQUEST

Pre-History

The stretch of the North Downs where Headley lies is believed to have been occupied since early prehistoric times, dating from several millennia ago. Stone Age remains from the Palaeolithic and Mesozoic periods have been found at nearby Walton-on-the-Hill and at Banstead Heath, suggesting that the high ground was preferred for settlement rather than perhaps the river valleys. The findings were of stone hand-axes and roughly-worked stone flakes.[1] Much of the Headley district was probably forested and though some open areas may have been occupied for a time a nomadic form of life was practised with hunting as the main activity. It is not known how many there were in any one group but that they were small is generally thought likely; each group presumably exploiting what was found to be available for food, moving on when these resources were exhausted.[2]

This form of activity is believed to have continued in the Headley and other North Downs areas for many centuries, into what is called the Neolithic period or New Stone Age. Some time ago a curved flint bar of this period, which may have been used as a hoe, was discovered near Headley and some small-scale implements dug up on Headley Heath, with others on sites at Walton-on-the-Hill.[3] At Pebblecombe, close to the edge of the parish boundary in the south, a Neolithic knife was found on a Clay-with-Flints deposit overlying the chalk at this poinr.[4]

The transition from the predominantly hunter-gatherers to small settlements with primitive farming developed in the Bronze Age (c. 2,500–800 BC) when knowledge of metal-working was being

brought into England by tribes from across the Channel. The archaeological evidence from this period for the North Downs area is slight.
The earliest settlement, close to Headley Heath, is believed to date
from the Late Bronze Age; a site here has yielded fragments of hand-
made pottery, animal bones, a worked flint and the broken point of
a bronze weapon.[5] It is thought that these flints suggest a small
enclosed settlement. Remains of hut circles have been found near
Headley and in areas nearby.[6]

Farming is not believed to have been undertaken, except in a
modest fashion, here and elsewhere in Surrey, until the Iron Age
(c. 800 BC to the beginning of the Christian era). Iron for tools
and weapons began to be used very early in this period, though the
change-over from bronze must have been gradual. Home crafts
developed, including the making of woollen fabrics, carpentry and
pottery.[7] Cereals were grown in many areas, the fields being near the
dwellings many of which had a timber fence round them as a form
of defence. Most of the farms kept cattle and sheep. Whether there
was a developed Iron Age settlement near Headley is not know but
future excavation may show one. If so, this might reveal evidence
similar to the well-developed Iron Age farming site at Hawks Head
in Fetcham. When the M25 motorway was being built in the 1980s
a small rubbish pit close to the Headley parish boundary near Stane
Street produced many fire-crackled flints, coarse pottery and part of
a conical loom-weight of baked clay. This suggests the presence of a
settled community.

Much of the new farming activity in the Iron Age, and the wide-
spread pottery making, resulted in part from the waves of immi-
grants, including the Celts and shortly before the Romans arrived,
the Belgae (Belgics). Both introduced fresh folklore and pagan
beliefs, including the making of more refined pottery and improved
artefacts.[8] 'Celtic' Fields (often square or rectangular), with their
upper and lower slopes defined by lynchets or small scarps, have
been recognised on Mickleham Downs.[9] East-West trackways were
followed close to the Downs by the tribes entering the country from
the Kent coast.

Headley under the Romans

The Roman invasion of England by the Emperor Claudius in 43 AD
is believed to have left the tribal units in most parts of the North
Downs (including Headley) largely unmolested so long as they

Fig. 6. A stretch of the Roman road, Stane Street, long overgrown, near Headley's western parish boundary.

accepted the Roman presence.[10] It was a very long period of occupation, lasting until 410 AD. During this time, despite many troubles in other parts of Britain, the farmers in the Surrey hills continued their pursuits of growing cereals and looking after livestock. Their prosperity, at least in mid-Roman times, may have blossomed with the likely need for more farm produce following the increase in the neighbouring urban population and the call for occasional supplies for the Roman Army. It is perhaps doubtful how much this swell if interest affected a small farming community like Headley.

There is no doubt, however, about the Roman presence in the Headley district, as revealed by archaeological sources. Roman tiles and broken pieces of earthenware have been found in the grounds of Headley Court.[11] Only a few miles away excavations have shown that there was sizeable Roman villa at Walton-on-the-Hill and another on Walton Heath. Roman pottery was found at both villas, some dating from early in the 1st century AD. They were occupied for a long time with evidence of some rebuilding late in the 4th century AD.[12] A Surrey Archaeological Society's report in 1999 noted that a concentration of Romano/British tiles had been observed in this area as well as a quantity of Roman pottery.

Further evidence of Roman activity in the Headley district is their construction of the important Stane Street road which in its alignment from Chichester to London passed near the western boundary

Fig. 7.   Roman coin. This was found close to Stane Street, not far from Headley. It is a silver denarius of the Emperor Alexander Severus, early 3rd century AD.

of the parish. This section of the road was originally surfaced with gravels, on a flint basis.[13] Close to Stane Street on its Headley side, numerous Roman coins were found during the layout of the Tyrells Wood Golf Course (they were mainly of the 3rd and 4th centuries);[14] only a few years ago a silver denarius of Alexander Severus (222–35 AD) was discovered near Stane Street (on one side of the coin is the head of the Emperor wearing a laurel wreath and on the other side is a figure of the goddess of the corn harvest, Annona).[15] The Ordnance Survey map of Roman Britain shows the roads (notably Stane Street) and the line of the trackways across or close to the North Downs, including also the north-south ones in and from the Wealden area. The trackways were probably made more useable by the Romans though their principal interests were the main cross-country highways.[16]

During the centuries of Roman occupation the Headley district is most likely to have absorbed the Roman way of life. A Romano/British cult certainly developed in the country and was firmly established to be maintained for a while after the Romans left in the early 5th century.[17]

The Saxon Years

The withdrawal of Roman troops ordered by the Emperor Honorius in 410 AD was soon followed by waves of Saxon and other tribes. Inter-tribal warfare was not uncommon. It is not thought that the invaders occupied the south of the county until well into the 6th century.[18] Day-to-day farming in places like Headley no doubt continued as in the past but trading of their goods probably declined now that the Roman markets were no more.

There are few signs of a Saxon presence in Headley. A Saxon burial site has been discovered alongside the line of Stane Street, found during the construction of some stables on the road to Headley.[19] There is, however, nothing comparable to the wealth of information obtained from the Saxon cemeteries at Ashtead and Leatherhead.[20]

Important developments in local rural administration were made in the late Saxon period. With the establishment of Christian worship, parishes were laid out and their boundaries settled. A group of parishes formed what they called Hundreds, Headley forming part of the Copthorne Hundred. The Courts of the Hundred met infrequently at an agreed central location and the site for the Copthorne one is believed to have been fairly close to the north of Headley near the ancient field name of Nutshambles.[21] Ecclesiastical administration was based on groups of 'minster' churches. There is no record of a church at Headley in the Saxon period, but the church known to have existed after the Norman Conquest (see p. 20) may have been built on or near the site of a Saxon one.

Notes

1. L.W. Carpenter; 'The Paleoliths of Walton & Banstead Heaths' *Procs LDLHS*, 1(10)1956, pp. 5–10
2. J & D.G. Bird; *Archaeology of Surrey to 1540* (1982) p. 66
3. D.C. Whimster, *Archaeology of Surrey* (1931) pp. 54, 230–8
4. J.Cotton, 'Neolithic Knives from N.E.Surrey' *SAC* (1984) pp. 225–33
5. VCH Surrey III (1911), p. 290
6. R.C. Elliott, 'The Banstead Story' *Surrey County Post* Oct. 1975
7. Barry Cunliffe, *Iron Age Britain* (1995), pp. 167, 265–96
8. L. Lang, *Celtic Britain* (1979) p. 10
9. S.S. Frere, 'Iron Age & Roman Sites on Mickleham Downs' *SAC* (1944/45), pp. 104–05
10. P. Salway, *Roman Britain* (1981) pp. 622 et seq.
11. A.W.G. Lowther, 'The Roman Period' *Procs LDLHS*, 2(2), 1958, p. 42

12. Ibid
13. A.W.G. Lowther, 'Roman Occupation' *Procs LDLHS*, I(4), 1950, p. 23
14. A.W.G. Lowther (1958) op. cit.
15. E.A. Crossland, 'Roman Coins Found' *Procs LDLHS* 5(6), 1993, p. 150
16. D.J. Turner, 'The North Downs Trackway' *SAC* (1980) p. 11
17. J.& D.G. Bird (1982) op. cit. pp. 165–96
18. R. Poulton, *Saxon Secrets in Surrey* (1990) p. 7
19. A.W.G. Lowther, 'The Saxon Period', *Procs LDLHS*, 2 (3), 1959, p. 72
20. J.C. Stuttard (ed), *History of Ashtead* (1995), pp. 20–2; Edwina Vardey (ed),
    History of Leatherhead (1988) p. 24
21. D. Nail, 'The Meeting Place of Copthorne Hundred' *SAC* (1965) pp. 44–53

Chapter 3

THE MIDDLE AGES

Headley Manor and its Medieval Owners

Twenty years after William the Conqueror defeated King Harold at the Battle of Hastings in 1066 the Domesday Book reported on towns and villages in the country, mainly for tax purposes. Accordingly to this, the manor of Headley (called Hallega) was held by Ralph de Felgeres, presumably one of the many knights or relations of the Conqueror who acquired land after Harold's defeat.[1] Many of the manorial landowners in Surrey and elsewhere after 1066 held several estates and would often be called away on the King's business. For this reason Stewards or Bailiffs were usually employed to look after their property or properties.

After referring to the Norman owner of Headley Manor the Domesday Book says that before the Conquest the manor had belonged to the Countess Goda (mother of King Harold), granted to her by King Edward the Confessor. It is not known how long Ralph de Felgeres held the manor but there are suggestions by some writers that Richard de Tonbridge (linked with Earls of Clare) later became the owner as he had of neighbouring Fetcham.[2] Indeed in the reign of King John it is known that in 1205 Headley Manor became for a few years under the Earl of Clare after a brief period held by Gilbert de Tyers.[3] Late in the 13th century, when Edward I was King, John de Plescy or Plecy, was the manor's owner and it remained in this family's tenure until 1363; after a gap, when Sir John Hamely held the manor, another Plescy took it over. The last male of this family died in 1417 and the manor was then subsequently divided, the most important part of which being owned by the Abbot of Westminster.[4]

Land Sales and Acquisitions

In the 13th and 14th centuries there was an active land market in Headley and also in the neighbouring parishes, probably due to a loosening of traditional manorial practices. Connected with this was the more readily availability of land at a time of greater prosperity, an additional factor being the proximity of London and its burgeoning market for country fare.[5] Sales of land were taking place even earlier, a late 12th century document referring to a grant of 'all the field of Wurthefeld' to someone in the village.[6] In 1218 Gilbert D'Abernon inherited through his wife part of the Lote estate here including 12 acres in a field called Potterscroft (with a grove in it), another 17 acres to the south of this and seven acres in Drews Field not far off as well as some 10 acres of wood 'Inname' to the west of this acquired land.[7] Later in the 13th century when John de Plescy owned the manor he rented out 40 acres to William de Ockle.[8]

The Lote, Legh and Wight families were among those building up mainly farming properties in Headley (and Leatherhead) over much of the 14th century and well into the next century. Documents from this period show how these families developed their interests, at times selling part of their holdings to friends or neighbours. Some of these deeds of exchange reveal interesting facts about the fields and layout of the farming land. In 1333 William ate Lote granted six acres of land to Laurence Wight in the north of the place called le Westfeld, abutting on John ate Legh's land 'next to Norestret'.[9] A few years later the same man granted his younger son land in Poterusfeld with hedges round it on the west; this plot bordered the road called le Lotstret and on the north was the pasture known as Leygrene.[10] In 1341 another landowner, John ate Nore, granted to John de Colnshurst of Mickleham a complete 'curtilage' called Le Bonheur adjoining Legh's tenancy.[11] Later in the 14th century the Wight family, which had London connections, acquired much land in Headley, but in 1420 their lands and tenements were passed to the Legh family in perpetuity.[12] So the Leghs were able to continue their long interests in the Headley area.

Farms and Farming

Headley was essentially a farming village in the Middle Ages as it had been in Saxon times ad would continue to be for many centuries, deriving benefit from its mixture of arable land and good pasture for livestock, though suffering in some respects from its high position rather cut off from lines of communication to trading centres. Self-sufficient farming was the general rule, at least in the early years after the Conquest, each farmer growing food for his family. An open-field system was operating at this time, under the manor's super-vision: the farmers, referred to in the Domesday Book as villeins, worked strips of land in the open-field (or fields) the land ploughed by teams of oxen; there were also a few men called bordars, small-holders often farming cleared or assarted land on the edge of the village.[13]

All or most of the farming community probably grew their crops in a three year rotation, fields being left fallow in the third year to maintain fertility, marl often being laid down to help this. In part of each week the farmers had to do labour services in the land of the ʰmanor's demesne, that is, those areas belonging specifically to the Lord of the Manor; this work entailed preparing the ground for crops, sowing, clearing of rubbish and harvesting.[14] The farming year was under the supervision of the Manor Court, but the controls in Headley (as in neighbouring Surrey parishes) were not so strict or limiting as the Midland counties of England.[15] Some control was, however, imposed on the crops sown and also on the times when sheep and cattle were allowed to feed on the stubble of arable land, as well as when villagers might raid the woodlands for firewood and their pigs be allowed to roam in the wasteland.

A glimpse of Headley's farming in the 13th and 14th centuries is shown by the following extracts from contemporary documents. In 1206 the manor was said to have 42 acres of corn, 12 oxen, 100 sheep, 13 hogs and one bullock.[16] A century later (1314) the arable land had increased to 75 acres and it had 10 acres of woodland with extensive pasture land in two large areas called Eldbury and La Or.[17] An Inqui-sition Post Mortem of 1358 revealed that 'two parts of the arable land within the manor's demesne would be sown each year if well tilled, the third part lying fallow for sheep pasture'.[18] The main crops in the demesne land and elsewhere were wheat and barley, with some oats; these would provide food for families, supplemented by meat from the cattle, sheep and pigs. The farmers also probably grew a few vegetables and some may have kept bees to provide honey for sweetening. The livestock were fed on the remains of the crops, the sheep's wool being used for simple weaving and, late in the period, for selling in neighbourhood markets.[19] Any excursions to these by horse and cart would have had to follow unpaved roads or trackways, often muddy after rain. The Gough map, dating from the mid-14th century shows a network of roads across Surrey and other counties.[20]

Farming and trade throughout the country suffered a great shock with the onset of the Black Death in the years 1348/49 when it is estimated that a third or more of the population of England died from it. Before this epidemic Headley's population was probably approaching 100 having increased somewhat during the recent prosperous years. A high proportion of Headley people must have succumbed to the Black Death. As in most other parts of the country this had the effect of gravely reducing the numbers of those working the land, fields being left untilled and not harvested. Farmers and landowners found it necessary to employ workers from outside the area. Labour shortages were one of the main causes of the Peasant Revolt in 1381, though it was the general dislike of the new Poll Tax which was its principal cause. Some Headley men may have joined the rebels since it is known that there were troubles within the county and a few from Surrey were reported to have supported the London mobs.[21]

Those taking part in the Peasant's Revolt, or supporting it, hoped for labour services on the manors to be abolished but despite much mayhem they failed to achieve this. However, in Headley and many other villages commuting of these services for money rents or in produce had begun to be increasingly common, as is suggested by the frequency of land sales and less stringency of the Manor Court.

The mid-15th century was another period of strife which the people of Headley probably had nothing to do with, though not far away, in Banstead, there were serious disturbances during Jack Cade's rebellion in 1450. The Wars of the Roses took place after this, but villages like Headley were all well away from any of the fighting.

Church and Parish
The earliest reference to a church in Headley is c. 1270. It may well have existed before this since its simple style, as known, suggests an early Norman or even Saxon construction, Though no church is mentioned in the Domesday Book the small settled population in the 11th century perhaps indicates that there may have been one here.[22] In 1291 a papal decree referred to Headley as being part of the Ewell Deanery.[23]

The medieval church was, it seems, built with only a nave and chancel, the west tower being added very much later at some time between the 13th and the early 16th century. A chancel arch was added in the 15th century with a Perpendicular East Window.[24]

The advowson, or the right to appoint the Rector, was for many years held by the Lord of the Manor, but from the early 15th century the Abbot of Westminster acquired it until the Dissolution of the Monasteries in the 1530s.

The Rector of Headley held some 15 acres of glebe land from which he produced food for his family. He also benefited from the grants of tithes.

Notes

1. J Morris (ed) *Domesday Book: Surrey* (1975), pp. 1, 5, 36
2. J.C. Stuttard (ed) *History of Fetcham* (1988), p. 14
3. VCH Surrey (1911), III, p. 290
4. E.W. Brayley, *History of Surrey* (1850) IV, p. 42
5. J. Blair, *Early Medieval Surrey* (1991), p. 35
6. J. Blair, 'Medieval Deeds of the Leatherhead District' *Procs LDLHS*, 4 (2), 1978, p. 35
7. CAF Meekings, 'D'Abernon Family before 1236' *SAC* (1980), p. 167
8. J. Blair (1986) op. cit. p. 270
9. J. Blair (1983) op. cit. pp. 178–81
10. Ibid, p. 179
11. Ibid, p. 179
12. Ibid, p. 181
13. Manning & Bray, *History of Surrey* (1809), II pp. 638–9
14. K.A. Bailey & J.C. Galbraith, 'Field Systems in Surrey', *SAC* (1973) p. 79
15. J. Blair (1991) op. cit., p. 82
16. Manning & Bray (1809) II op. cit. pp. 638–69
17. Ibid
18. Ibid
19. F.E. Huggett, *A Short History of Farming* (1970), pp. 7–10
20. R.A. Pelham, 'The Gough Map' *Geog. Journal* (1993), p. 34
21. E.B. Fryde, *The Great Revolt of 1381* (1981), pp. 14–15
22. J. Blair, 'The Destroyed Medieval Church at Headley' *Procs LDLHS*, 4(2), 1978, pp. 39–44
23. VCH Surrey (1909) II, p. 49
24. J. Blair (1978) op. cit., p. 40

Chapter 4

THE TUDOR AND STUART YEARS

The accession of Henry VII in 1485 as the first Tudor King is often registered as the end of the Middle Ages and the beginning of early modern times. However, for the people of Headley this was just another year of working in the fields though it is known that good harvest weather then and for several years after this assured a welcome to the new king.[1] At Headley and all other farming areas the weather was always crucial to the success of the crops upon which the villagers depended for their livelihood. They could not have foreseen, of course, the political, social and religious reforms which were to affect their lives in the years to come. Headley, like other parishes, had to get used to a series of dictats from the government of the day for much of the early 16th century to about the mid-17th century, though this was a period, however, when the standard of living improved in both town and country. Shakespeare and many other famous poets and dramatists lived at this time, notably in Queen Elizabeth's reign. Some of the more well-to-do Headley residents may have found their way to see a Shakespeare play at the Globe Theatre in London.

Manorial Ownership
The Abbot of Westminster held Headley Manor at the beginning of Henry VII's reign, but in the 1530s when Henry VIII was on the throne the Dissolution of the Monasteries led to the manor here being taken over by the Crown.[2] The ownership was soon passed to Andrew, Lord Windsor but after his death it came into the possession of Lady Ann Knyett in 1578. Fifteen years later William Stydolf became the owner and advowson holder, settling it upon his

wife; the Stydolfs also had wide family interests in the Mickleham, Ashtead and Leatherhead areas. The family maintained their ownership of Headley Manor until early in the 18th century, leasing it out on several occasions.[3]

Farming Ways, Old and New

The loosening of the manorial system ties, already advanced here in the Middle Ages, continued, with the villeinage tenure giving place to more copyholds and free-holding. There were still many open fields, but fields with hedges, that is, enclosures, were becoming more common, especially when new land was being developed in the waste and forested areas. Crop shortages in some years, because of the weather, often persuaded the farmer to extend his land where possible, perhaps also turning more to livestock as a source of profit.

The Manor Court continued to watch over most farming activities. In Queen Elizabeth's reign the Court frequently disapproved of farmers 'encroaching and enclosing land'; and in 1612 the Court complained of 'fences between fields at the land called Le Nore and Le Homefield'.[4] A few years earlier the Court was insisting that the farmers working on the manor's demesne should 'keepe their swine out of the common field from 18th October until the fields be broken up' and another order about the same time regulated 'the keeping of ducks and geese on Turner Pond'. Yet another order, in 1614, included the 'imposition of fines on inhabitants who did not keep fences and hedges in good order' (suggesting that many fields in Headley were now enclosed rather than open); at the same sitting the Court passed an order on the pasturing of sheep (presumably restricting their being allowed to enter the crop-growing fields until after the harvest), the offenders having to pay a fine to the Lord of the Manor and a small declared sum to the poor of the parish. At a Surrey Quarter Sessions in 1666 there was a complaint that a gate had been out of repair between Headley Heath and Box Hill, allowing cattle to stray and so 'destroy the corn'. From all these records it is clear that, despite land tenures being easier there was still much control over farming ways.

Something of the character of Headley farming in the late 16th century is revealed by the Inventory of the farmer John Hays who died in August 1578.[5] The whereabouts of his farmhouse and farm are not given, except that they are 'in the parish of Headley.' The Inventory in fact says little about his home, referring mainly to his

'featherbed' and 'flockbed', with 'pairs of blankets', bolsters, sheets
and coverlets; also he had two table cloths 'of canvas' and, in the
kitchen four candlesticks, two kettles, a pair of pothooks and pothan-
gers, as well as three dozen trenchers (wooden platters). Hays clearly
lived modestly, though a reference to his holding a dozen or more
of pewter vessels indicates perhaps a certain affluence. His holdings
at the farm are of particular interest; there were 16lbs of wool in the
barn and among his livestock there were 100 wethers (rams), 40 ewes
and the same number of lambs, five calves, five heifers, four bullocks,
seven 'kyne' (cows), and four oxen. Of cereals grown only 16 acres
under oats are mentioned, with some rye. Miscellaneous farm
belongings, kept on or near the farmyard, included five horses (two
mares, an old horse and two colts), 14 geese, six ducks and 'other
poultry'; a cart 'with a pair of wheels', a plough, some shovels and
'other old iron'.

Despite the emphasis on livestock in Hays' Inventory there is little
doubt that most Headley farms still pursued mixed farming, as in the
past, growing mainly wheat, barley and oats, with sheep grazing on
the Downs and some cattle in favourable locations. John Norton in
his 1595 book *The Shires of England* speaks highly of the corn being
grown on the slopes of the North Downs.[6] The appreciation by an
acknowledged authority may have encouraged Headley farmers to
read one or more of the farming books then widely available.

It was not only books which persuaded the countryman to
improve and enjoy his farming tasks. Headley farmers, like many
others, may have derived much pleasure and encouragement from
Nicholas Breton who (in about 1626) sang happily about country
life:[7] 'Oh, to see a faire morning, or on a summer evening lambs and
rabbits running, the birds billing and the flowers budding. . . . Who
would not think that the brightness of a faire day doth not reveal all
the beauties of the world.' In another passage he waxes eloquently
on the delights of rural life: 'For pleasure we rise with the lark and
go to bed with the lamb. . . . We have hay in the barns, horses in the
stable, oxen in the stalls, sheep in the pen, hogges in the stye, corn
in the granary, cheese in the loft, milke in the dairye, whole cloths
to our backs, some money in the coffers and having all this what in
God's name can we deserve to have more.'[8] Let us hope that these
lyrical passages reflect something of the flavour of country life at
Headley in the early 17th century.

Population and Occupations

At the beginning of the Tudor period Headley's population was perhaps only in the range of 50-100, based on the 1524 Lay Subsidy
returns,[9] taking into account those not then included, notably
women, children and servants. This total is rather more than was
recorded in the Domesday Book,[10] but there would have been many
fluctuations since then with the numbers building up until the devas-
tation of the Black Death in 1349/50 (see p. 20),[11] slowly increasing
after this to its Tudor level. There was no marked change in the
Archdeacon of Surrey's return in 1603,[12] but the population showed
a slight increase at the time of the Hearth Tax (1664)[13] and in the
returns made for William III's Association Oath Roll near the end
of the century.[14] The names of the signatories to this provide a rough
record of those living in Headley at this time:

Association Oath Roll, 1695

John Hilary (Rector)	William Burkett
Andrew Weller	Michael Summers
John Treggm	Robert Weller
Mark Studland	Thos. Margetts
Richard Bridger	William Lucas
Richard Easted	Thos. Kemp
Thos. Barker	Benjamin Flint
Thos. Moor	Thos. Lee
Richard Dixon	John Weller
Robert Hiskin	John Chapman
John King	Francis Dixon
George Frank	Matthew Dimond
Thos. King	Thos. Benge
Thos. Hammond	Erasmus Rumse
Edward Nettlefold	John Lucas (Constable)
William Gerois	Henry Ireland
George Gillatt	Robert Roffee
Thomas Pullen	John Hubbard
John Hatcher	William Heath
	William Kemp

All heads of Headley households may not have subscribed to the
oath required but since most of them probably did it seems fair to
suggest that the population of the village (including women, children
and servants) was most likely to be about 175 in 1695.

Farming was the main occupation of most Headley residents, supported by some carpenters, wheelwrights and blacksmiths. Weaving

was probably carried on in the home, using wool from sheep on the Downs. There is no record of any local brewery, though a few homes may have brewed their own ale.

It was common practice in those days for fathers to send one or more of their sons to train in a neighbouring town. In 1662, Robert Nettleford of Headley was sent by his father for a seven year's apprenticeship to Thomas Gowldwyer, a Kingston mercer; and in 1670, another Nettleford, son of Edward, a yeoman, began a similar number of years as an apprentice in Kingston to William Hall, a barber.[15]

Church Reforms

In the early years of Tudor rule the church at Headley, like others in the country, continued their services and customs as in the past, but Henry VIII's break with Rome in the mid-1530s led to many doctrinal and other changes. Bibles in English were ordered to be placed in every church in 1536 and in 1538 the first stage of dismantling the relics began.

The pace of reforms increased with the accession of Edward VI in 1547. Headley Church and others elsewhere had to use the first English Prayer Book which was printed in 1549. About the same time an Inventory of the church's possessions was made for eventual sale to the Crown; and in 1553 most of these were ordered to be seized. Among the items taken were two altar cloths, two brass candlesticks, three vestments of embroidered silk, a 'braunched' cope, some surplices, a cross of copper and gilt, a pair of brass sensors, a holder for holy water and two bells.[16]

Another Inventory of quite a different kind survives from this period; dating from 1551 it lists in detail the goods and belongings of the late Rector of Headley, Sir William Lythgo, as shown below:[17]

Fedder (Feather) bed, Shirts and Towels, Three candlesticks, Four platters, Three small dishes of pewter and a pewter pot, Cubborde (Cupboard), Rownde(Round) table, Coffer, Saddell (saddle) and Bridle, Short gowne of London Russett, Gowne of London town, Two other short gownes, Two wolstyde (worsted) jackets), Doublet and three pairs of hose, All the Boyckes (Books), Money in the purse.

Sir William Lythgo seems to have lived modestly at his Headley Rectory.

After the death of Edward VI in 1553 Lythgo's successor had to cope with Queen Mary's ruling that the Catholic rites should again be followed, but this was for a short period only because in 1558 Queen Elizabeth came to the throne. The Protestant rubric was re-introduced and Headley Church (like all others) had to accept the display of the Thirty-Nine Articles of Religion also the Creed. The old stone altar had to be replaced by a wooden table. The changes imposed by Queen Elizabeth were perhaps not so extensive as those earlier in the century but they were severe enough to worry the congregation and the Rector. During James I's reign, the Ten Commandments had to be displayed at the East End of every church, in 1604, and seven years later, all parishes received a copy of the Authorised Version of the Bible.

Soon after the outbreak of the Civil War in 1642 Parliament acted swiftly to clear the country of parish priests whom they believed to be recalcitrants or opponents of Presbyterianism. To this end they ejected many priests, including, in 1644, the Rector of Headley, Andrew Tarrant, and the living was sequestered to Henry Dallender, later to John Massey.[18] Other steps taken by Parliament at this time included the abolition of episcopacy and the insistence that the new Directory of Worship should replace the Book of Common Prayer

Fig. 8. The Old Cottage, Tot Hill. This probably dates from the early 16th century, with modern additions (see p. 84).

Fig. 9.   Heather Cottage, in lane off Tot Hill. When first built in the late 17th century there were three cottages on this site (see p. 85).

in all church services. Parliament was also active in these years against landowners who were regarded as 'delinquents', that is, those suspected of assisting the Royal cause: such a man was William Stydolf, Esquire of the Royal Bodyguard and owner of Headley Manor, who was fined the then large sum of £1,746 in 1649 by the Parliamentary Committee involved in these matters.[19]

Before the William Stydolf case came to be considered the Commons had passed an Ordinance for the establishment of a parochial Presbyterian system in the country.[20] The so-called 'Classical System' for Surrey was sanctioned in February 1648 and Headley, with many other neighbouring parishes, was included in the Dorking 'Classis'; ministers and elders were required to be nominated.[21] There was no special success in establishing these 'classis' and it is believed that most country Rectors or Vicars may well have managed to carry on without undue pressures to introduce changes. They could not, however, avoid accepting the particularly unwelcome Parliamentary decree in September 1653 that all marriages should be civil ones only, before a J.P.; and it was also decreed about this time that the main Christian festivals should no longer be observed.

With all these unpopular strictures imposed by Cromwell's Parliament in the 1650's it is not surprising that Charles II's return in 1660 was widely celebrated in town and country. Soon after the Restoration Richard Wyld was instated as Rector of Headley and so far as is known he and later Rectors had no major disputes with London to contend with. Wyld's successor was John Hilary, who became an Archdeacon when at Headley, staying as incumbent until 1710.

Parish Life

The church, apart from its religious role, had for long been important in the social life of the village, but this was strengthened in the late 16th century when the Vestry was given extra administrative responsibilities. The Vestry group was made up of the Rector, the two churchwardens and several prominent members of the community. In 1555 they were made responsible for road repairs, a Surveyor of the Roads ensuring that every man of the village did six days of road repair work every year. The Vestry also selected someone from the village to be the Constable; apart from keeping order he collected what taxes there were and was responsible for taking local reprobates to appear before the Justices of the Peace. In his hands also was the call-up of Headley men to join the Surrey musters at the time of the Spanish Armada threat in 1588.[22] An equally important figure in the Vestry was the one elected to be Overseer of the Poor who looked after those in need, a task made more demanding by the Elizabethan Poor Law Acts of 1598 and 1601.

At several times during the early Stuart years there were pleas from the government for the rural parishes to help this or that cause. Contemporary records show that William Stydolf of Headley, he who was to be arraigned for 'delinquency' in the Civil War, paid in 1625 the then large sum of £20 to aid the King in his war with Spain;[23] only 'persons of good means' were approached by the Lord Lieutenant of the County for this purpose. Nine years later Headley had to pay a small sum to the unpopular Ship Money tax of Charles I;[24] and, on the eve of the Civil War in 1642 they offered a similar contribution to the Relief of Protestant Refugees from Ireland.[25] After the Restoration in 1660 the parish responded to a call from London for a 'Free and Voluntary Present to Charles II'.[26] In the 17th century's

later years Headley was able to settle down to its normal activities
without undue pleas or interferences from London, except for William III's 'Association Oath' call in 1695 (see p. 25).

Notes

1. W.G. Hoskins, 'Harvest Fluctuations, 1480–1619' *Agric. Hist. Rev.* (1964) p. 39
2. F.W. Brayley, *History of Surrey* (1850) IV, p. 421
3. Manning and Bray, *History of Surrey* (1809) II, pp. 638–9
4. Headley Manor Court Rolls: *SHC* 439/1
5. Inventory: H.W.1578, B.44/2: Transcribed by Marion Herridge
6. J. Norden, *The Shires of England* (1595): BL, Add Mss 31853
7. Nicholas Breton, *The Twelve Months* (1626) BL
8. Ibid, *The Court and Country* (1613) BL
9. PRO: E 179/133/122
10. J. Morris, *Domesday Book: Surrey* (1975), pp. 1, 5, 36
11. P. Ziegler, *The Black Death* (1954) p. 230
12. BL: Harleian Mss, 595
13. C.A.F. Meekings, *Surrey Hearth Tax* (1940)
14. *Association Oath Roll* , 1695, W Surrey FHS Record Series
15. Ann Daly, *Kingston upon Thames Register of Apprentices*, 1568–1713 (1974)
16. R.A. Robert's 'Inventories of Edward VI's reign' *SAC* (1908) p. 5
17. Inventory of Sir William Lythgo (1551): HW, B.86. Transcribed by Marion Herridge
18. H.E. Malden, *Rectors & Vicars of Surrey Parishes* (1914), pp. 9–10
19. Cal. SPD, Committee of Compounding (1649) BL
20. VCH Surrey II (1911), p. 35; W.A. Shaw, *History of the English Church, 1640–1660* (1900)
21. *Surrey Past & Present* (1971) p. 101
22. 'Surrey Musters' *SRS* (1914) pp. 6, 150
23. A.R. Bax, 'Loan to Charles I' (1625) *SAC* (1902) p. 81
24. VCH Surrey II (1911) p. 442
25. 'Surrey Contributions to the Relief of Protestant Refugees from Ireland' (1642) PRO:SP28/194: transcribed by Cliff Webb , 1982
26. 'Free & Voluntary Present to Charles II, 1661/62' W. Surrey FHS Record Series (1982)

Chapter 5

THE GEORGIAN PERIOD

After the turmoil of the Stuart period – civil war, political upheaval and religious intolerance – the arrival of the Hanoverian dynasty must have seemed like an oasis of tranquillity. George I and his successors may not have been greatly loved but they provided some stability in both politics and religion; so the ordinary country folk of Headley, not affected by political and religious manoeuvring, could live and work again according to their old family traditions.[1]

Early in the 18th century, in the reign of Queen Anne, one of the worst storms ever recorded struck Headley and much of Southern England. John Evelyn asserted that at its peak on 26/27 November 1703 large numbers of trees were blown down in the district, and Daniel Defoe wrote about it in a book entitled *The Great Storm*. Many churches lost their spire, including the St Mary and St Nicholas Parish Church, Leatherhead.[2]

In 1720, Headley might have been significantly affected if a proposal had been pursued by Arthur Moore of Fetcham Park to construct a long classical style building divided into separate dwellings (of the kind seen in London and Bath squares). The architect was John Price and the site was to be the common fields of the manor.[3] The project might have been linked with the spa at Epsom Wells, but the spa's loss of popularity and Arthur Moore's death in 1730 may explain why only two dwellings were said to be finished in 1736.

The Manor of Headley

In 1710, on Sigismond Stydolf's death, his wife, Margaret, inherited the manor. Margaret then married Michael Hyde, and later Thomas Edwin, who inherited on Margaret's death in 1734. Thomas died in

Fig. 10. Housing Terrace Project, 1720. It was never completed[3].

1735, and the manor passed to the family of his nephew, Charles Edwin and then to Edwin's nephew, Charles Windham, who took the name of Edwin; he sold the manor in 1784 to Henry Boulton, who lived at Thorncroft in Leatherhead. With a fine house in Leatherhead, it does not seem surprising that Henry Boulton sold his Headley house to Colonel Alexander Hume, who took the name of Evelyn after his marriage to a daughter of William Evelyn of St (Clare/Cleer)? in Kent. Colonel Evelyn sold the house to Robert Ladbroke, who purchased the rest of the estate from Henry Boulton in 1804.[4] Sale particulars for the manor in 1803 show that there were nearly 1100 acres for sale, comprising:-

The Manor & Court-house Farm	(447 acres)
Slough Farm	(278 acres)
Heath Farm	(124 acres)
Other land in Headley	(181 acres)
Land in Ashtead and Walton	(49 acres)

There were also seven houses with small plots of land.[5]

Soon afterwards the estate (but not the house) was sold to Richard Howard of Ashtead. His heir, Mary, married the Hon. Fulk Greville Upton, who took the name of Howard on marriage. She survived her husband and lived on well into the Victorian era.

Headley Grove

This small estate grew up around a modest property originally known as 'Tiewood' later 'Tyeland', as a result of well-to-do investors moving out of London in the 18th century. A substantial collection of deeds and documents[6] shows that, in 1704, Edward Thurland of Reigate leased for 60 years a run-down timber-framed building, with a few outbuildings and 14 acres of land, to Sir John St Leger of the Inner Temple; Sir John, having spent £300 on the property assigned the lease to John Taylor in 1716. Andrew Percivall was assigned the lease of Tiewood (Tyeland) in 1723, and Thomas and Margaret Edwin (the Lord and Lady of the Manor) leased three acres of Headley Heath to him in 1725. On Andrew Percivall's death, the lease was assigned to Mary Prinn (née Percivall), and after her death in 1760 her executors sold the estate to George Udney, a London merchant.

Precisely when the freehold of 'Tiewood/Tyeland' changed hands is unclear, but it seems to have been in the hands of George Udney when his nephew, William Fraser, inherited it by his will in 1771.

William acquired 62 acres of woodland and pasture from Charles Edwin, the Lord of the Manor, in 1781. He took the name of Udney and left the property to his aunt, Mary Udney, by his will in 1793; she left it to Major General Alexander Mackenzie Fraser by her will in 1808. As he was posted overseas, he sold the estate, then known as Headley Grove, to William Ritchie in 1809.

In 1813, after the Brockham and East Betchworth Inclosure Act of 1812, William Ritchie bought land in Betchworth which he exchanged in 1817 for five acres, owned by the Duke of Norfolk, as the duke's land was nearer to Headley Grove House; in the same year he acquired three acres from Richard Howard, the Lord of the Manor. William's executors sold Headley Grove House with 93 acres of land to Felix Ladbroke in 1828. By the end of the 19th century the estate had grown to about 113 acres.

Farms and Farming

It has been estimated that about half of all arable land was already enclosed as fields with hedges by the beginning of the 18th century[7]. In Headley there might have been some manorial land still farmed under the 'open field' system and certainly there was further enclosure of common land during the 1700s. Manor Court Rolls refer to the enclosure of manorial wastes (1741); to proposals by tenants to give up their rights in Le Nower in exchange for enfranchisement of tenant's estates from heriots (1788); and to encroachment on the Heath (1799).[8] There were several farms of at least 100 acres in Headley by the 1800s – sale particulars for the Manor refer to Courthouse, Slough and Heath farms, and particulars for Headley Grove estate also refer to a farm.[9]

A definitive map of 1706 gives details of Waltonhurst Farm, which was owned then by Arthur Moore of Fetcham. This arable farm comprised about 100 acres in Walton-on-the-Hill and about 60 acres in Headley on its northern border.[10] In 1719, Moore obtained a lease for 1000 years from Mrs Hyde, the Lord of the Manor, giving him the right to take water from the vicinity of the Nower; in particular he was entitled to pipe water to any part of the farm.[11] When Arthur Moore died in 1730, his son, William, sold the Fetcham estate and lived at Polesden House where he died in 1746. His executors had to seek an Act of Parliament to enable them to sell his estates to pay off his debts.

The papers kept by the principal executor, Francis, Lord North, provide some information about the farm at that time. The tenant, Mr Richbell, seems to have been in arrears with his rent in 1748; Zebedee Lovemoore, William's factor, writes to Lord North – 'have been to Mr Richbell's at Headley ... he has promised to make up £20 for rent .. '.[12] There are several references to payments of rent by Philip Richbell between 1750 and 1753 which seem to relate to annual rent of £37. The farm was sold by the executors to Richard Jackson in 1755 for the sum of £1067.5s.[13] By the Victorian era, the farm had been broken up and the land in Headley had become part of the park attached to Headley House (later called Headley Park).

The Church

Headley Parish Church in the Georgian period, apart from several new monuments in the tower, remained much as it was in earlier centuries (see Chapter 3); its squat buttressed tower at the west end of a short nave and chancel, dominated the village. In the 1820's, Charles Cracklow published an external view of the church and his ground plan suggests that it was about 60ft long and about 25ft wide. His view from the south-east shows a three light window in the buttressed east wall of the chancel, a small single light in the south wall of the nave near the chancel arch, and a two light Tudor-framed window nearer the centre of the same wall. If the north wall of the nave had similar windows and the tower had only small louvre windows at the top then the inside of the church must have been rather dark and dismal even with candlelight. The communion plate was 18th century – a standing paten (1706) and a cup (1752).

There were only four rectors appointed during the whole of the Georgian period:-

John Nason served for 33 years	1710–1743
Andrew Wood served for 28 years	1743–1771
Jonathan Morgan served for 47 years	1771–1818
Lewis Sneyd AM served for 8 years	1819–1827

After Sneyd went to Oxford, there was an interregnum until the appointment of Ferdinand Faithfull in 1830.

Although this was a period when authority of the Anglican Church was having to accept a growth in independent non-conformist meetings in many parts of England, the Bishop's Visi-

Fig. 11.   Headley Parish Church, 1823, an engraving by W.T. Cracklow.

tations in 1725 and 1788 state that there were no non-conformists in Headley.[14]

Schools
In the Georgian period, a sound classical education was a necessary requirement for a gentleman. So it is not too surprising that there was a private school in Headley. It appears that, at some time after 1691, the Rev Ambrose Bonwicke established such a school[15] and Manning and Bray mention the existence of a school, before 1722, run by him.[16] In 1725, the Bishop's Visitation reports – 'No public school; only a private one consisting of gentlemen's sons. The present master, Mr Stubbs. Scholars about 20 in number'. No school is referred to in the 1788 Visitation.

The Village Community

Headley was still a small isolated community in the Georgian period. Although demographic studies indicate that the nation's population fluctuated at the beginning of the 18th century due to outbreaks of disease, it had increased by about 50% by the end of the century. Headley's population, however, remained dormant at 'about 200 souls' at the Bishop's Visitations of 1725 and 1788, and '217 inhabitants' at the first census in 1801. John Rocque's map of 1770 shows that Headley's isolation did not benefit from the road improvements which followed the spread of turnpike roads throughout England after the Turnpike Act of 1755.[17]

Some smaller properties in Headley are referred to in sporadic deeds, viz: messuages called Cottell (1718), Westfield (1734), Painters (1757), Gibbons (1789) and one called Palmers (1809).[18] The Manor Court Rolls for 1770 refer to the consent of tenants to William Rowland for the building of a shop and premises on manorial waste 'near a place known by the Sign of the Cock'; this probably relates to the Cock Inn; Petty Sessions minutes certainly refer to alehouse licences granted to the Cock and the Coach and Horses later in the century.[19]

The pound, an enclosure for animals, stood near the 'Sign of the Cock' and the Manor Court Rolls refer to its derelict state in the 1780s; also the need for stocks to be put up near the pound.

Fig. 12. The Cock Inn, 1825.

An inventory shows that William Burchett's possessions were valued at £50 when he died in 1784. He had lived in a copyhold property in Headley valued at £40, but also owned a freehold one in Dorking occupied by a tenant, Mr Standbridge, who paid an annual rent of £10. All William's other possessions – cash, clothes and furnishings of his bedroom. kitchen, pantry and barn – were valued at £5.[20]

The poor did benefit sometimes from the wills of the rich, but there could be restrictions. When the Rev. Ambrose Bonwicke died in 1722, his will gave money 'to be divided between the poor of Headley and of the parish where I shall be buried to be distributed among such persons only who usually frequent their parish church and have therein received the Holy Sacrament within a twelve month before the time of such distribution, unless disabled by some bodily infirmity'.[21] The Manor Court Rolls for 1753 indicate that the poor house built on the waste 'is very ruinous for want of repair' and in 1790, the Petty Sessions ordered the overseers (Alexander Hume Esq and Thomas Charrington) to answer why they had failed to help three of their poor.[22]

When James Edwards, a leading Land Surveyor, visited Headley in the 1780s he described it as 'a small straggling village on a hill with a pleasant Heath of about 1,000 acres.' After referring to the Rectory as being in the gift of H. Boulton Esq he gave several lines to what he calls Headley Hall (later to become Headley Park) lying 'north of the church'. Other records suggest that this property was built about 1800, so Edwards may well have written about it shortly before 1801 when his book was first published. He described it as a 'large modern building, the seat of Alexander Hume Esq.' A spring in Nower Wood provided the house with water – which Edwards thought remarkable because of its 'lofty eminence'. Just west of the Hall was Headley Court, a large farmhouse owned by H. Boulton, Esq. and occupied by a farmer called Charrington.[23]

At the end of the 18th century, the renewal of war with France caused some concern about a possible invasion and both towns and villages were encouraged to set up 'Armed Associations' to assist in their defence. This idea was soon superseded by a more formal proposal for organised units of volunteer infantry and cavalry similar to the militia. A real threat of invasion by Napoleon arose in 1803 and each county was told to find a given number of volunteers, which was 1,781 for Surrey. A Surrey military assessment in 1805 showed a shortage of 1,010 men and fines were levied on parishes based on a figure of £20 per deficient man. Headley was fined £1.18.04 (about the same as Ashtead and Fetcham, but less than Great Bookham and Mickleham). The growth of British naval power soon removed the threat of invasion and the fines were probably never collected.[24]

After the defeat of Napoleon in 1815, the high price of corn, which had benefited farming communities during wartime, fell and laws were introduced to control the import of foreign corn; nevertheless, the cost of bread rose and wages fell, and riots occurred in 1830 in counties south of the Thames and elsewhere. Farming conditions, helped by good harvests and advances in technology, improved in the late 1830s up to and after the accession of Queen Victoria in 1837.

Notes

1. J.H. Plumb, *The First Four Georges* (1956) Ch 1 The Georgian World
2. D. Defoe, *The Great Storm* (1703): BL
3. F.B. Benger, 'A Headley Building Project of 1720', *Procs LDLHS*, 3(3), 1969, p. 78; for the engraving of the proposed building see *Procs LDLHS* 4(7), 1983, p. 197
4. VCH Surrey (1911), 3, p. 291; Manning & Bray (1809), II p. 637; Brayley 1870, 4 part 2, p. 419
5. SHC 85/2/1/1/18
6. SHC 3760 (see also *Procs LDLHS*, 5, 1990, pp. 86–96)
7. W.G. Hoskins, *The Making of the English Landscape* (1985) pp. 177–8
8. SHC 439/8
9. SHC 85/2/1/2/18
10. SHC 822/1
11. SHC G97/13/574
12. *North Papers*, d2, f36; Bodleian Library
13. *Raymond Richards Collection*, N7/1; N7/2 and N 9/5; Univ. of Keele
14. SRS vol XXXIV (1994), pp. 34, 114
15. SAC vol 13, p. 115
16. Manning & Bray (1809) II, p. 809
17. P. Langford, *Eighteenth Century Britain* (2000)
18. SHC 2714/1/37/4; 2714/1/37/5; 2714/1/37/7; 6187/5/1 and 203/20/1
19. W Surrey FHS Record Series 8
20. PRO: PROB 31/733/745
21. SAC vol 13, p. 116
22. W Surrey FHS Record Series 8, p. 38
23. J. Edwards, *Companion from London to Brighthelmstone* (1801) (see also extract in *Procs LDLHS*, 5, 1994, p. 190)
24. SAC vol 52 pp. 60–65 (see also *Procs LDLHS*, 5 (4) 1991, pp. 103–5)

Chapter 6

THE VICTORIAN AGE

Early Years

For rural communities like Headley the early and middle periods of Queen Victoria's reign from 1837 to about 1870 were for the most part prosperous, the mid-Victorian years sometimes being called the 'Golden Age' of farming. There were several good harvests in these years, especially in 1849, 1855 and 1868; the price of wheat was about 55s per quarter at the beginning of the reign in 1837, achieving a high of 74s in 1855.[1] These good prices and the many fine harvests would certainly have been welcomed by the Headley farmers.

Some of the good feelings generated early in the reign were helped not only by the more than satisfactory agricultural returns but also by the reforms which had been made on tithe payments. A tithe or tenth of all produce from the land had for centuries been given to the church each year. The call for a cash equivalent had been growing for some time (especially during the early 1830s) and this was made compulsory by the Tithe Commutation Act of 1836; tithes were converted into payments based on the prevailing price of grain.[2] At the time of these tithe changes the main landowners were the Hon. Fulk Greville Howard, husband of Mary Howard (of Ashtead Park), with 788 acres and Felix Ladbroke, with 273 acres; most of the 17 others had under 10 acres each.

Although these landowners and their tenant farmers were most probably making good profits from the land there were still some restrictions on their actions by the Headley Manor Court. Complaints were frequently made by the Court about footpaths being impassable, the failure to repair fences and the obstruction of roads. The right of depasturing cattle and sheep on the wastes of the Manor

continued to be restricted; and permission had to be sought from the
Court to enclose pieces of manorial land.[3]

The Farming Surveys of 1866 and 1873
In the mid-Victorian years the government in London showed a special interest in finding out what products were being grown and the
numbers of livestock held in the rural areas, also the ownership of
the farming land.[4] The main farms in Headley at this time were:
Court Farm, Heath Farm, Hurst Farm (partly in the Walton-on-the-
Hill parish) and Slough Farm.

The 1866 returns for Headley are given in the following table:

Agricultural Returns, 1866

Crops	Acres	Crops	Acres
Wheat	1,212	Potatoes	6
Barley	725	Turnips/Swedes	68
Oats	116	Mangolds	1
Rye	32	Carrots	2
Peas	3	Cabbages	
Lucerne	10	& other vegs.	8
Clover	157		

Bare fallow or uncropped arable land   45 acres
Permanent Pasture, Meadow (excluding hill pastures)   254 acres

Livestock
Milk Cows: 33; Other cattle: 31; Sheep: 1,569; Pigs: 65.

The table shows the great variety of crops grown in Headley and
the preponderance of sheep among the livestock. A few cows are said
to have been kept by the Rector and the Cock Inn.

The 1873 survey was a 'Return of Owners of Land' rather than of
farming details,[5]

Headley Landowners, 1873

Owner	Acreage
Mrs Bordier	107
James Bridges	1
H. Carew	3
Samuel Gurney	63
George Holliday	1
William Jones	7
Henry Knight	14
Jane Lee	1
George Lyall	566

John R Phillips	179	
William Pullen	5	
The Rector	15	(The Glebe)
The Common (including Headley Heath)	489	
	1,451	

After these returns were made an agricultural depression soon developed throughout the country with cereal and wool prices falling dramatically, caused by the arrival of large US imports. A series of poor harvests did not help and in the late 1870s there was a serious outbreak of sheep-rot. Headley's mixed farming of pasture and arable land probably improved the viability of its farms during these difficult years. Wheat prices fell as low as 22s a quarter in 1894 but there was some recovery at the turn of the century.[6]

Ownership of Headley Manor

For much of Queen Victoria's reign Headley Manor was owned by the Howard family of Ashtead Park. Mary Howard and her husband Col. Fulk Greville Howard (né Upton) held this property since 1819, but in view of their wide interests elsewhere (at Ashtead, Castle Rising in Norfolk, Elford House in Staffordshire and Levens Hall near Kendal) it is unlikely that they were able to spend much time at Headley. As at the other properties a Steward probably carried the bulk of the responsibility for running the estate. This would almost certainly have been the case after Col. Howard died in 1846.[7]

When Mary Howard died in 1877 Headley Manor first passed to her cousin and heir Major-General Bagot and after his death a few years later it was purchased by the Hon. Henry Dudley Ryder, soon to become the 4th Earl of Harrowby.

The Parish Church, Old and New

In the 1850s it was decided to pull down the old medieval parish church (see p. 20) and build a new one. Cracklow's fine sketch of the old church in 1824 shows it looking well on the hill-top site (see Fig. 11) but according to the 1851 Religious Census there was 'insufficient accommodation' for the size of the congregation and it was also reported to be 'rather dilapidated' about this time.[8]

Work on the new building – the present church – began in 1855

Fig. 13.   Headley Grove, early 19th century. Courtesy, S.A.S. Collection.

slightly to the north of the medieval structure; the former site being
marked by the lines of the clipped yews in the churchyard. The construction of the new church was finished in 1858 and it was conse-
crated by the Bishop of Winchester in August 1860. The church was
built in the 13th century style, the tower and spire becoming a local
landmark, as they are now. G.E. Street was the architect for the chancel and the tower, Anthony Salvin for the nave: both were well-
known Victorian architects. The bowl and cover of the font, and
King Charles II's Royal Coat of Arms, given by Mary Stydolf in
1666, were preserved and placed in the new church.[9]

At the time when the new church was built the Rector of Headley
was the Rev Ferdinand Faithfull who had been the incumbent since
1830. When he died in 1871 a memorial to him was constructed close
to the south porch of the church, built from the rubble of the old
church.[10]

In February 1892 sermons were given by the Rector, the Rev
R.L.J. Chamberlain to commemorate the life of the great preacher,
C.H. Spurgeon. The Rector was a close friend of Spurgeon who had
recently died.[11]

Fig. 14. Parish Church and School, late 19th century.

Fig. 15. Headley House, Tilley Lane, a mid-19th century engraving. The house was burnt down in 1896 and when rebuilt became known as Headley Park. Courtesy, S.A.S. Collection.

Evangelical Chapel

This chapel, made of corrugated iron and sometimes called the Mission Hall or Tin Tabernacle, was built in 1888 on Headley Heath. Its services were well attended for many years, to which the preachers and organist used to come up to Headley by pony, cycle and donkey cart. The chapel's popularity lessened at the turn of the century and it closed down in 1908.

Schools and Schooling

The mid-19th century was an active period for the setting up of schools at Headley.[12] Although only a small village there were as many as five schools founded during these years, sharply divided by social class. A 'Preparatory School for Young Gentlemen' was run by the Rev Ferdinand Faithfull soon after he was appointed Rector in 1830; it was held on the top floor of the Rectory and was attended by about 20 boys from four to twenty years of age. In the 1850s there was a 'Select Boarding School for Young Ladies' at the Gar-

Fig. 16. Memorial Arch, St Mary's churchyard. This is in memory of the Rev. Ferdinand Faithfull, who died in 1871.

dener's Cottage in the Headley Park grounds. This was open to 'tradesman's daughters'. The youngest of the 'labourers' children (two to five years) were taught at Crabtree Cottage; slightly older children had their lessons at Wood Cottage. From eight years onwards the boys went to a school in Ashtead while the girls at this age were sent to Mrs Ladbroke's school at a wooden building in the village. A description of this relates that 'Some of the older children swept and sanded the floors and, in winter, they lit the fire with a red-hot poker taken from Mrs Ladbroke's man'. The main subject taught was needlework, though reading writing and arithmetic were also in the syllabus.

Soon after Mrs Ladbroke left the district in 1858 her school and most of the others were incorporated in the new Church of England School built during the 1860s, supported by a Government grant and by voluntary subscriptions. It was a mixed school for about 80 pupils and it soon became popular in the village.

Late in the 19th century the Surrey County Council opened in Headley what was called by them a 'Continuation School', set up to give the local children a measure of further education. It was not particularly successful, closing down after a few years.

Craftsmen and Traders

It is not surprising that most of the craftsmen in the Victorian years were associated with country activities, as they had been in past centuries. The shoemaker, George Braithwaite, was also a shopkeeper and postmaster and, in addition, there were carpenters and wheelwrights. A forge close to Oyster Hill was kept busy for most of the year, particularly during the Epsom races when horses were brought here to be shod. However, late in the 19th century much of the work tended to be in wrought iron commissions from large houses and from London.

The Kelly Directories late in Queen Victoria's reign[13] refer to a Surgeon working at Headley in 1887, to a painter in business here in 1891 and to a builder in 1895, evidence perhaps for some new building activity in the area.

Craftsmanship and employment of quite a different kind should be mentioned here by a reference to the important life and work of Emily Faithfull, daughter of the Rev. Ferdinand Faithfull, the Rector of Headley. She was born in 1835 and distinguished herself late in life by becoming Printer and Publisher-in-Ordinary to Queen Victoria. In 1860 she had successfully founded the Queen Victoria Press in London in which the compositors were 911 females. Her lifetimes' aim was to extend the sphere of women in work. She died in 1895.[14]

Postal Services

Headley had its first official postal services in 1845 when in February that year George Matthews, landlord of the Cock Inn, became Receiver of Posts. The Post Office business stayed here until the late 1860's, William Moore, a grocer and blacksmith, becoming the Receiver. Julia Braithwaite, also a grocer, took over the position in 1881, her brother succeeding her in the late 1880s. About this time letters arrived from Epsom at 8.20 a.m. and 11.30 a.m.; they were dispatched at 1.40 p.m. and 5.50 p.m. On the wall at Headley Park there is a Victorian wall-box manufactured between 1881 and 1904.[15]

For most of the Victorian years only stamps or postal orders were sold at the Headley post office,[16] the nearest money order and telegraph office being at Walton-on-the-Hill. However, a telegraph office opened at Headley in the early 1890s, though a telephone exchange had to wait until 1912.

Village Administration

For most of the 19th century the bulk of Headley's village life, apart from the Manor Court work, was handled by the Vestry. As in past centuries, its members collected the church rates and dealt with local administrative problems. Road repairs were also a concern of the Vestry. The roads round Headley were modest only, not like the neighbouring turnpikes around Ashtead, Fetcham and Leatherhead. The roads serving Headley were very much the same as they were shown on the Rocque map of 1770[17] and on the Ordnance Survey map of 1816. The Vestry's concern for the roads must have been a continuing and exacting undertaking.

The responsibilities of the Vestry were all changed when its civil duties, as distinct from its religious ones, passed to a newly formed Parish Council when the Local Government Act became law in 1894. One of Headley's Council members served on the Epsom Rural District Council. The influence of the Surrey County Council, founded in 1888, was also being felt in rural areas like Headley.[18]

The Headley Parish Council, like the Vestry before, was responsible, among its many other tasks, for the distribution of charity money. Each year since the early 17th century money was received, as in many other parishes, from the Henry Smith Charity and this still continues. For an account of Henry Smith's Charity see Ernest Crossland's two articles in *Procs LDLHS*, 5 (9), 1966, pp. 230–3; and 6(3), 1999, pp. 56–61.

Sport and Games

Cricket: A Cricket Club was first formed at Headley in 1862 on ground given by Mary Howard the then owner of Headley Manor but because of indifferent support it soon closed down. However, the club was re-founded in 1893 and it has continued up to the present day (see pp. 65–7). A Ladies v Gentlemen's match was played in 1896.

Football: There had been talk in the village since the early 1860s that there should be a football club but this had to wait until October 1899 for its foundation. During its early years matches were played against Ashtead, West Humble and Brockham, sometimes with the Rector of Headley in the team. For the club's later history see p. 67.

The Social Scene
It is difficult to convey a true and full picture of Headley life during the long reign of Queen Victoria. The population of the village changed little in these years, from 322 at the 1851 Census to 394 in 1901. There were no doubt the usual festive occasions at Christmas, Easter and the New Year, also at harvest time, especially in the good years as they were so often in the first 25 years or more of the Queen's reign. In its very early days the only public house was the Cock Inn, but in 1846 the Claremont Inn was built and soon became a welcome meeting place during the rest of the century and beyond; it was named after a race horse and it used to provide private stabling for horses during the Epsom race meetings. Guy Fawkes Day, 5th November, was usually celebrated with fireworks and a bonfire.

In the early 1860s the new Church of England school-rooms were used for club meetings, concerts and lectures, but these were transferred to the Reading Room after it was opened in 1882.

There was an active and popular Gardener's Society in the late 19th century with annual shows in the gardens of one of the large

Fig. 17. Claremont Inn, Tot Hill.

houses.[19] These houses held occasional garden parties for the villagers
in addition to the ones for the Gardener's Society. The Lyall family
of Headley Park, Sir John Bridge of Headley Grove, Walter Cunliffe
(later Lord Cunliffe) of Headley Court and the Ryders of High
Ashurst took an active interest in the village and its welfare.

Near the end of the century there were exciting celebrations at
Headley, as elsewhere in the country, to mark Queen Victoria's Dia-
mond Jubilee on 22nd June 1897. After a special service at St Mary's
Church and the ringing of bells the activities later in the day took
place in the grounds of Headley Grove. There were sports for all
ages, dancing in a marquee during the evening and a bonfire after
dark. Music accompaniments were given by a string band and the
Headley Drum and Fife Band.

There was soon to be a change of mood with the outbreak of the
Boer War in 1899. Headley, like other parishes, offered comforts for
the troops and bells were rung here and everywhere on the Relief of
Mafeking in May 1900.[20] There was general sorrow on the death of
Queen Victoria early in 1901.

Notes

 1. J.M. Stratton, *Agricultural Records* (1977) pp. 106–15
 2. SHC: Headley Tithes and Map, 1840
 3. SHC: 439/9, Headley Manor Minute Book, 1820–95
 4. PRO: MAF 68: Surrey
 5. West Surrey FHS: Record Series, 1995
 6. J.M. Stratton (1977) op. cit. p. 118
 7. SHC: 439/9 op. cit.
 8. *The 1851 Religious Census: Surrey*, SRS 1997, pp. 110–11
 9. W.J. Blair, 'The Destroyed Medieval Church at Headley' *Procs LDLHS*, 4(2),
    1978, pp. 39–44
10. W.I. Scrapbook (1965)
11. SHC:6187/5/1: Headley Parish Records
12. W.I. Scrapbook (1965)
13. Kelly Directories for 1887, 1891, 1898
14. E. Ratcliffe, *The Caxton of her Age* (1993)
15. P. Tarplee, *A Guide to the Industrial History of Mole Valley* (1995), p. 70
16. W.I. Scrapbook (1965)
17. SHC, M2/9/2
18. W.I. Scrapbook (1965)
19. SHC, 6187/5/1
20. *Leatherhead Advertiser*; report on the Boer War

Chapter 7

HEADLEY IN THE 20th CENTURY, AND TODAY

Introduction

During the course of the 20th century Headley remained small in population and successfully resisted the trend to semi-urbanisation. There were many difficulties facing life here, as elsewhere, during the two wars of 1914–18 and 1939–45 and the years between the wars were at times economically stressful, especially in the early 1930s. After the trials of the last war Headley settled down to the peacetime years, becoming near the century's end less of a farming village than it used to be but still a much admired rural community.

The First 20 Years: Peace and War

In the first few years of the new century life in Headley continued its quiet way, though the many national 'events' were commemorated or celebrated. When Queen Victoria died in 1901 a Service of Commemoration was held in her honour and muffled bells were rung. The next year celebrations took place in the village to mark the Coronation of King Edward VII and in the same year (June 1902) the church bells sounded a Victory Peal to mark the end of the Boer War; flags were flown on this day, as they had been on 24th May when the government established Empire Day for the first time. Two more national occasions were observed by Headley in the next few years: these were the funeral of King Edward VII in 1910 and the Coronation of King George V a year later.

As for Headley itself during these early years of the 20th century, perhaps the most important event was the building and opening of the Village Institute (later known as the Village Hall). The foundation stone was laid by the Dowager Countess of Harrowby on 23rd May

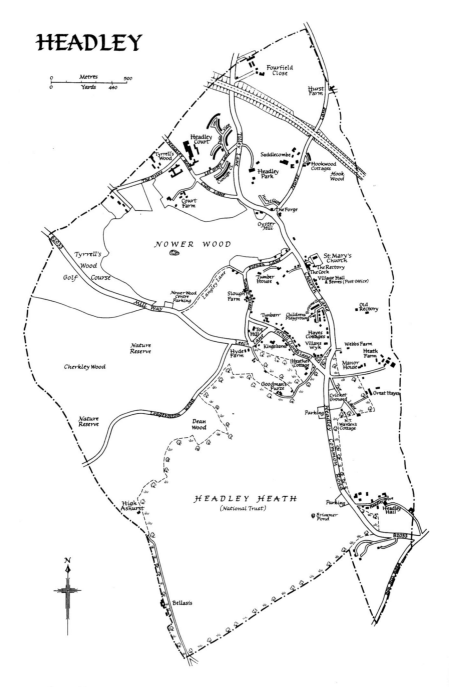

HEADLEY

Map of Headley. *Courtesy, Headley Parish Council.*

1903 and it was soon to become the main social centre for the village. Only a year later a Working Men's Club was founded which met regularly at a room in the Village Institute. A few years before this (1898) the banker, Walter Cunliffe, was completing the building of his large new home, Headley Court, on or close to the site of an old farmhouse; he was particularly concerned with helping life in the village and the Village Institute gained much from his generosity. Cunliffe was made Governor of the Bank of England in 1913 and during the next year was raised to the peerage.

When the Rector of Headley, the Rev P.M. Barnard resigned in October 1905 the living was sequestered for about four months; before the Rev C.J. Vernon succeeded as Rector in February 1906 the church duties in the interim period were undertaken by masters from St John's School in Leatherhead.

In the century's first decade the government of the day authorised a number of social measures, affecting all: in 1908 pensions for the old were made law and three years later Lloyd George's Insurance Act introduced the doctor's panel and the insurance stamp, seeking to help the poor and those in need. In the same year (1911) a half-day holiday for shops was passed by Parliament.

There was little to suggest in rural areas like Headley that the clouds of the First World War (the Great War) would soon be arriving and even if some villagers may have suspected that there was some good evidence for this, no-one would have guessed its four year length. When the war came in August 1914 farming at Headley and other country areas had, of course, to be carried on to supply the nation's food in a crisis. Crop levels were encouraged to be increased during the war years. It is not clear how many troops came to or passed through Headley but there were large numbers in neighbouring Ashtead. To protect farmers, so important in wartime, the local Commander issued an Order that 'great care is to be taken by troops of all arms when training to avoid doing damage to wheat and young seeds; and they must also keep a distance for sheep folds and lambing pens.'

Early in 1916 conscription was introduced for all men between 18 and 41. A Surrey Volunteers Regiment was however reported to be in camp at Headley in August of that year. There were food shortages over the country in 1917, though the Surrey War Agricultural Committee had extended their orders for farmers to extend their normal crop-growing areas.

Fig. 18. School pupils, 1917. The staff and pupils are going to the Rectory for tea on Empire Day.

Many young Headley men were called to the colours and 11 lost their lives on military service; they are remembered in a Roll of Honour at the parish church. After the end of the war in November 1918 the nation-wide Peace Celebrations took place in July 1919. At Headley a special service was held at St Mary's Church and bells were rung; later in the day there were sports and fireworks.

During the middle years of the war, in 1916, the Rev T.E.R. Phillips was appointed Rector of Headley and he was the incumbent here for the next 25 years. He had been recognized internationally for a long time as a distinguished astronomer, having been elected a member of the British Astronomical Association in 1896 when he was 28 years old and later, in 1899, a Fellow of the Royal Astronomical Society, becoming its President. At Headley he soon set up two observatories at the Rectory with three large telescopes. Most of the leading astronomers of the day, including the Astronomer Royal, used to attend his annual garden party at the Rectory. Phillips was a popular priest during the remaining years of the war and in the peace that followed.

Fig. 19. Rev T.E.R. Phillips, Rector 1916–41. He was a distinguished astronomer.

Fig. 20. Phillips' Observatories in the Rectory grounds.

Between the Wars

In the early 1920s Headley, like other parts of the country, was still recovering from the exigencies of war. Its trials were remembered when in September 1921 in the parish church a War Memorial was unveiled by Major-General Sir Edmund Ironside: the names of the Headley men killed in the war are inscribed on a tablet, and there is another tablet like it in the Village Hall.

The Headley Manor Court continued to assert its authority in the post-war years, including many cases where a copyholder sought and usually achieved enfranchisement, after the 1922 Act had abolished this form of tenant farming; there had been some lessening of the copyright laws in 1894 but the later Act made the tenure illegal. The phrase used in the Act and repeated in the Court records is that these lands 'be for ever discharged from all fines, heriots and other controls'. The Headley farmers holding land by copyright would certainly have welcomed this new law affecting them, being introduced at the same time when the price of wheat in the market was quite high and remained so until the late 1920s.

A further, wholly different, concern of the Manor Court at this time was overseeing the laying of electric cables in parts of Headley; the village had first received limited electricity in 1902. It was agreed

Fig. 21. Shop and Village Hall in the 1930s.

by the Court in June 1920, acting for the then Lord of the Manor (H.M. Crookenden) that the Leatherhead & District Electricity Company should be allowed to lay underground cables in the manorial waste ground at Oyster Hill and also at the side of Church Lane. This was, according to the Court records 'for the purpose of erecting and maintaining two transformer sub-chambers in connection with the supply of electric cable to the parish of Headley'. The cables passed along Leech Lane and Lodge Bottom Road to Mickleham, also along Tilley Lane to Headley Court and so to Ashtead and Leatherhead.

Since 1922 a Headley Choral Society, including some from the village school, competed at the Leith Hill Musical Festival, under Vaughan Williams, and at the 1925 one it was particularly successful in gaining the banner for sight-reading and for part-songs. The Society also achieved 2nd place in the madrigal competition.

Headley was probably little directly affected by the countrywide industrial troubles which led to the General Strike of 1926. However, some of the villagers may have slipped into Dorking or Leatherhead to help volunteers to drive buses and other vehicles.

After a somewhat restrictive life in the war years the Headley School flourished in the 1920s. There were ups and downs in the attendance figures, especially in the summer months when the Derby and other races were being held at Epsom, the parents taking their children there. Sir Arthur Glyn, a leading education figure, fairly often came to the school and talked to the students. The girls took their cookery classes at Walton-on-the-Hill and once when they complained that a stalker was in the woods a police escort was provided for them for a week or two. In the early years of the century the pupils of the school had been permitted by Lord Cunliffe of Headley Court to use the swimming pool at his house and this privilege was continued by Lady Cunliffe after her husband had died in 1920. On some occasions in the 1920s the school was closed when it was used as a polling station for the Epsom Division.

The opening of the 1930s was a grim time for many parts of the country in the wake of an economic depression, sparked off by the Wall Street crash in 1929. Rural areas like Headley were unlikely to have suffered as much as the towns, though wheat prices fell sharply in 1932 and 1933 and remained low for the rest of the decade. To help the farmers the government passed an Import Duties Act in 1932, imposing duties on agricultural imports, except from British countries overseas. Two years later milk was ordered to be supplied free to all schools. Despite the economic downturn in the 1930s this was also the time of rapid housebuilding and increased population in Ashtead, Fetcham and Leatherhead, whereas Headley had no development on this scale, with only a limited population increase. The attraction of these neighbouring places for new residents was mainly due to their having good railway and road connections, especially with London.

Cricket and football continued to be popular during these years. In June 1931 the Headley cricket team was honoured with a visit to their ground by A.E.R. Gilligan, the former English Captain and member of the Sussex Club. He was on an arranged tour of English village cricket clubs and Headley was the first to be visited. A match was played and it was reported in the *News Chronicle*. Crowds attended this match which added appreciably to the popularity of the Club. The Headley Football Club was equally well supported at this time, playing matches at Headley Park and at various fields in the village; coaches were hired for away matches. In 1936/7 the Headley team were winners of the Dorking League.

The mid-1930s were marked by several occasions when Headley followed the nation's tributes to and celebrations of the Royal family. In early May 1935 there was a general holiday for the Silver Jubilee of King George V, welcomed by the children of the Village School and by others. When the King died in the following year a commemoration service was held at St Mary's Church; and, after the abdication of King Edward VIII, the Coronation of King George VI was celebrated.

There was little feeling in Headley or elsewhere that another war was imminent, though there were warnings in the press and some suggestions of a need for a training in air raid precautions. Life, in fact, carried on more or less as before. As late as 7th June 1939 Headley held a fête in the beautiful gardens of Headley Court, by courtesy of the Dowager Lady Cunliffe. There was country dancing round a maypole, many sideshows and an indoor concert. Three months later the Second World War began.

The Second World War
After the outbreak of war in September 1939 Headley like all other places had to get used to many restrictions, including the use of gas masks, curtains on house windows to meet the black-out provisions,

and a shortage of petrol. Food rationing was begun in January 1940 covering butter, bacon and ham, sugar being added a little later. In July the same year tea was reduced to 2 oz per person per week, quite a blow for many families. The farmers of Headley, like those in other rural areas, were encouraged to grow more wheat and oats, also potatoes. The newly formed Women's Land Army had a hostel in Farm Lane, Ashtead and the girls there may well have helped the Headley farmers.

Early in the war the Dowager Lady Cunliffe gave up her owner-ship of Headley Court and it was soon requisitioned by the wartime government for use as the headquarters of the Canadian troops in this area. They were at Headley Court from 1942 to the end of the war. Their activities on Headley were considerable. Military training of many kinds took place here, mainly on Headley Heath, including the building of a trench system dug on the slope opposite Middle Hill. All parts of the Heath were traversed by track vehicles when tactical exercises were carried out. These churned up the ground, made worse when a Wellington bomber crash-landed here on one night. North of the Headley Cricket Ground members of the Royal Observer Corps set up a viewing point for observing and recording the movement of planes. Not far from the Cricket Ground there was an airstrip, able to handle light aircraft, which was used for some of the operations undertaken by the Special Operations Executive, or SOE, centred at Bellasis. This house, on the south-western edge of Headley Heath, was taken over by the government early in the war. It is now privately owned.

Soon after the Dunkirk evacuation during the spring of 1940, in which two Headley men were involved and returned safely, a series of enemy raids started. There were numerous alerts in Headley, notably in the months September to December that year but no casu-alties occurred. The Headmaster of the Village School was advised that when an air raid warning was sounded all the children should go for safety into the parish church. Col. S.L. Bibby, a Headley resi-dent, raised and commanded a local Home Guard battalion over a wide area and in 1943 he was County Commandant of the Surrey Army Cadet Force which he held until after the end of the war. Bibby later became Deputy Lord Lieutenant and High Sheriff of Surrey.

In August 1941 the Rector of Headley, the Rev. J.F.O. Lewis, reported that he had been asked to act as Food Organizer for Head-

Fig. 22.   Headley Court. *Courtesy, Defence Services Medical Rehabilitation Centre.*

ley in the event of an invasion. 'Iron Rations', sufficient to feed the
parish for ten days, were stored at the Rectory and at Heath House.
No invasion, of course, took place but this instruction to the Rector
(no doubt widely circulated elsewhere) gives a clear indication of the
government's view of a possible invasion at this time.

There was a singular, temporary relief from the anxieties of the
war late in 1942 when the church bells throughout the country were
allowed to be rung – the only time in the war - to celebrate the Battle
of Alamein in October of that year. A little earlier than this the
Village School had adopted the Royal Navy warship 'The Lune'.

Another series of air raids began in 1944 and on 2nd July Headley's Rectory was severely damaged by a flying bomb. The Rector
and his family were in the building at the time of the bombing but
they all escaped unscathed.

During the course of the war about 90 HE and flying bombs fell
on or close to Headley, also a number of incendiary bombs, mainly
around Fairfield Close. There were fortunately no casualties. The
German aircraft were presumably offloading their bombs after a
sortie over towns and military installations. On a clear day the bal-

loon barrage giving protection from these air raids was a fine sight
from St Mary's churchyard.

There must have been more than the usual military activities by
the Canadian troops at Headley Court in the weeks and months
before the Allied invasion of Europe early in June 1944. After the
Allied victory in the spring of 1945 VE Day was celebrated throughout the country. St Mary's Church at Headley had a Thanksgiving
Service with bells ringing at the end; the village was decorated with
flags and in the evening a bonfire was lighted on Tothill. There were
similar celebrations on VJ Day in September 1945.

About 75 Headley men served in the forces during the war. Three
of these lost their lives and after the war a tablet was placed in St
Mary's Church in memory of them.

Peacetime Again: The First Ten Years, 1945–55

At the end of the war in 1945 Headley and everywhere else expected
a return to better times, but this was not to be for a number of years.
Food and clothing continued to be rationed and a coal shortage
added to life's difficulties. It was not all gloom, however; Headley's
returning soldiers enlivened the village helping to make family life
normal again. On the rationing front, things did not improve since
in 1946 bread was added to the 'restricted' list of foods for the first
time. The Leatherhead & District Food Control Committee had a
brief to watch over food supplies in the villages round Leatherhead,
including a distribution of numerous gifts of food boxes from
Australia.

The austerity of these early post-war years is further shown by
the near impossibility of buying new cars (until about 1953), the
scarcity of luxuries, and the limitations of foreign travel because of
severe currency restrictions. The extremely cold 1947 winter with
blizzards from January to March did not help Headley's spirits. The
government's formation of the National Health Service in 1948 was
generally welcomed and in the same year life was helped by the lift-
ing of the bread rationing, with clothing also no longer restricted in
1949.

When the Canadian troops moved out of Headley Court after the
war it was bought in 1946 by the Institute of Chartered Auction-
eers & Estate Agents, which then presented the house and grounds
to the RAF to commemorate the Battle of Britain (for the later history of Headley Court see p. 65). In the same year Headley Heath

was given by Mr. & Mrs. Crookenden of Headley Manor to the National Trust (the Trust also thereby acquired the Lordship of Headley Manor).

The year 1948 will be remembered in Headley because of the death of the famous motorist, Sir Malcolm Campbell. He had bought Headley Grove in the 1930s and was well known in the village. His most popular sports car was 'The Blue Bird'.

Some Headley people will recall the 1950s as the period when peacetime truly returned, with the availability of new cars, nylon stockings in the shops and the easing of travel abroad. They will also probably remember one or more of the plays, like 'Quiet Weekend' and 'Sailor Beware', performed by the Headley Amateur Dramatic Club, founded in 1948; their productions were all very popular and on one occasion they were invited to the RAF at Headley Court, after which the RAF helped the Club in many ways.

This was the time of the exhilarating Festival of Britain, 1951, and some of the villagers, perhaps a good number of them, found their way to see all or most of the exciting things the Festival had to offer.

The Coronation of Queen Elizabeth II soon followed the Festival of Britain and on Coronation Day, 2nd June 1953, Headley had a special celebratory service at St Mary's Church and in the afternoon there were sports at the Cricket Ground, with a large Children's Party at the Village Hall. There was dancing in the evening and the church was floodlit.

Two years later, in early July 1955, St Mary's Church celebrated its centenary in fine fashion. The walls of the church were floodlit; 'the combination of light and shadow with the rugged flat walls and the nearby trees' provided a splendid picture in the summer dusk. At the service on 3rd July the Bishop of Guildford, the Rt Rev H.C. Montgomery-Campbell and the Rector, the Rev B.R. Lloyd-Jones, referred to the old church and how the new one replaced it in 1855 (see p. 42). A week after the service there was a performance of Handel's 'Messiah', the church choir being augmented by the St George's Singers of Ashtead and by girls from Parsons Mead School.

Farming after the War
In the years after 1945 farming conditions at Headley were generally most favourable, with high crop yields and good prices in the market. This was the position in a number of the following years. Traditional farming, however, was to become much less generally followed in

the later years of the century. Before these changes occurred the farms were still largely functioning as they had been for a long time.

Of Headley's five farms after the war *Heath Farm* was probably the largest, its fields stretching behind Oyster Hill and the Church, but the farm buildings were on the left of the road leading up to the Heath. It was managed by Mr. Alford for Mr. Wates (of The Manor House). There were about 215 acres of arable land and 200 more of woodland, with soil ranging from the quick-drying sandy variety near the Heath to Clay-with-Flints in the lower fields. The crops grown were: 20 acres of wheat, 40 acres of barley, 20 acres of oats and 5 acres of kale. The wheat was sold but the other corn was for feed. The farm had a herd of about 60 Guernseys for milk purposes and a beef herd of 50 Herefords; about 250 poultry were also kept, mainly for domestic use. Hay and straw were baled to be stored under cover or in stacks sheltered from the rain by lashed-down netting. Four men were employed at Heath Farm, three living in modern homes built in Church Lane and one at the farm itself.

Headley Park Farm was run by the tenant farmer Mr Walton, with the help of only one young man. Apart from its 70 acres some ground in Ashtead was rented, partly to help replace some of the original farm land that then housed a riding stable. This farm kept the only sheep in Headley at this time (250 in 1965); they also held some poultry. The crops sown included 25 acres wheat, 35 acres barley, both for sale, plus a small patch of kale and turnips for sheep feed. The rest of the ground was kept for grass.

Slough Farm housed about 80 milkers (Jerseys) and it also had a beef herd of 50 Aberdeen Angus. *Hyde Farm* grew wheat, barley and oats, as did the others. At *Tumber Farm* pigs were the main interest; they were kept in modern concrete stalls.

A sixth farm, *Warren Farm*, almost all of which lay outside the Headley border, looked after a milking herd of about 50 Friesians.

The activity of these farms was to change a great deal before the end of the century.

Headley in the last 35 years to the Millennium (1955–2000)
During the remaining years of the 20th century Headley's farming, which used to be so important, became no longer so, as already mentioned above. Elements of farming still continue, but Headley has become a more purely residential area than hitherto. The development of housing has been restricted by the fact that Headley lies

within the Green Belt, imposed by the Town & Country Planning Act of 1947. Some Council houses were, however, built in 1951–2 at Broome Close and pre-1967 at Hookwood (they are now mainly privately owned). A few of the larger houses in the village have been converted into flats. The parish church of St Mary has maintained its pastoral care, as always, and has celebrated many local and national festive occasions with special services. Henry Smith's charity donations continue (see p. 48), as they have done for a long period. A further charity, the Braithwaite Trust, has recently been formed, for the upkeep of the church and its churchyard.

During the early 1980s the owner of *Heath Farm* and the tenants of *Tumber*, *Slough* and *Hyde Farms* died and as neither were family farms the sons did not take over the running of the farms and the stock and equipment were sold off. A speculator who tried to sell the land off in small leisure plots bought the land at *Heath Farm*. The Council successfully resisted this and the land was gradually broken up into units used to graze the increasing number of horses stabled in the area.

Tumber Farm was sold off in two lots and the land used for 'horse-culture'; one of these establishments now rents the majority of the land that was *Hyde Farm* and uses it to graze horses at livery and a few pet cows.

Farms in Headley,
2000

Heath Farm	Livery Stables
Tumber House Farm	Grazing
Tumber Lodge Farm	Livery Stables and a few pet cows. Hay crop.
Hyde Farm	Horse paddocks and the barns are used for general storage.
Slough Farm	Private House, including yard and buildings.
Addlestead Farm	Livery Stables
Warren Farm	Owned by the National Trust. There are some sheep and cattle, also arable crops. The land is let out to a tenant farmer and the buildings are National Trust offices and Workshops.
Headley Grove Farm	Livery Stables

Headley Court Defence Services Medical Rehabilitation Centre

After the acquisition of Headley Court by the RAF in 1946 the fine house built by the Cunliffe family in 1898 was soon to be used as a rehabilitation unit. A whole series of special buildings for this purpose were erected in the large and beautiful gardens of the house. The house itself came to be used as the Officers' Mess, and for general purpose also.

The buildings are well spaced in the grounds and consist of a remedial block, physiotherapy and occupational therapy departments, as well as medical and administrative departments. There is a fine and large swimming pool, more accurately called a 'Hydrotherapy Pool' since it is used to assist physically and mentally impaired patients with movement.

For most of the years since 1946 the RAF was the only Service operating at Headley Court, but in 1999/2000 the Ministry of Defence decided that the Royal Navy and the Army should be fully represented as well. The RAF flag which used to fly here is now replaced by the Ministry of Defence one.

Headley and the M25

There had been plans before the Second World War for a major road, the South Orbital (later to be the M25) to pass over Headley Heath but this was 'put on the shelf' until after the end of the war. In 1967 the plan resurfaced and there was soon strong local opposition to the road's proposed route through Headley Heath and close to Headley village. Representations were made to the Inspector appointed by the Minister of Transport, opinion in the village differing somewhat on where the line of the motorway might be. It was felt that the Heath and the village would be seriously damaged if the plans for the M25 in this area were not changed. After some delay Headley's approach was accepted by the government. It was agreed that the M25 would follow a more northerly route than originally planned, some distance away from Headley village and its Heath, though a short stretch crosses the extreme north of the parish. The M25 opened on 6th October 1985.

Sport and Leisure

Cricket: The Headley Cricket Club soon revived after its wartime closure, beginning a series of matches on its fine ground adjoining

Fig. 23. Cricket match at Headley, early 1980s. *Courtesy, Sir Michael and Lady Pickard.*

the Heath. Many of these were against clubs outside the area. For many years a match against a Treasury team was played, arranged by Edward (later Lord) Bridges, who lived in Headley. For three successive years late in the 1950s Terry Thomas, the well-known actor, brought teams to Headley consisting of stars from the stage and screen, radio and television. Crowds flocked to see these matches. In 1960, the Surrey County team came to Headley in a Tony Lock memorial match. The Club has continued to flourish.

Although many of the players come from outside Headley there is considerable support within the village. The upkeep of the ground on Headley Heath is a credit to the club and home games attract many spectators. The Club runs two teams: a Saturday and a Sunday team with the Sunday one always playing at home. The Club celebrated its centenary in 1993 by staging a year of special events.

Football: The Headley Football Club, refounded after the war, had some successful seasons in the early years. The 1953/4 season was the most rewarding one in its history when Headley won both the Dorking League and the Sportsmanship Cups. Unfortunately, a few years later, in 1957, the Club had to close down, because of player shortages, funding problems and the lack of proper facilities.

Horseriding: Since the last war horseriding has become enormously popular and the demand for stabling has taken over all the available farm buildings. Owners visit daily to tend their animals. The good riding available on Headley Heath and the surrounding countryside makes continuous demands for stabling and something like saturation point has been reached. The main stables are Headley Park Farm, Tumber Lodge Farm, Headley Grove, Saddlecombe and Headley Trace with many residents owning horses with stabling or horse shelters adjoining the houses. Loretta Lodge right on the Headley boundary is a racing stable with full training facilities. Local riders have formed a group called Headley Heath Riders Association to promote good riding practice, the welfare of horses and to raise money to maintain the bridleway network.

Sports at High Ashurst: This Sport and Educuation Centre, run by the Surrey County Council, is on the western edge of the Headley parish boundary. A large number of sports are pursued here, including archery, rope courses, orienteering, camping skills, mountain

Fig. 24.   Riding on the Heath.

biking and environmental education. The Centre occupies the site of the former High Ashurst Mansion built in the 19th century.

Golf: The Tyrells Wood Golf Course, near the western border of Headley parish, occupies a large estate once owned by the Cunliffe family who also built the nearby Headley Court. Golf was first played here in the early 1920s when the Keswick family were owners of the estate. The Club's first Captain was Sir Ronald Blades, MP for Epsom, later Lord Mayor of London, becoming Lord Ebbisham in 1928. In 1999 the Club celebrated its 75th anniversary. The Tyrells Wood Golf Course has long been admired for its greens and handsome Club House.

Film Making: Over the years since the war the Heath has been used in the making of a number of films. These have included scenes from 'Albert RN', 'Dr Finlay's Casebook', 'The Three Musketeers' and 'Moonstrike'.

Fig. 25.   Entrance to Saddlecombe Stables.

Meeting Places

The *Village Hall*, built in 1903, was in its early years called 'The Institute', becoming known by its present name in 1919. It has been a popular venue for all manner of social engagements and functions ever since. The *Post Office*, with its shop, lies immediately next-door to the Hall and a small café has recently been added to it. Only a few yards away is *The Cock Inn* (now named *The Cock Horse*), built in the 18th century but very much changed since then. There used to be another public house in Headley, known as *The Claremont*, named after a racehorse; it was a well-known village meeting place, but in 1958 it was sold and turned into a private house.

Some Days to Remember

New Bells at St Mary's Church, 3rd May 1966: The Bishop of Guildford, Dr George Reindorp, dedicated Headley's chime of seven

Fig. 26. Headley Forge, close to Oyster Hill. As it was in the early 1990s. *Courtesy, Steven Scobell.*

Fig. 27. Tyrells Wood Golf Club. A view of the Club House.

new bells and the 15th century Hille bell from Rye in Sussex from the original chime. The new bells replaced the original ones installed when the church was built which had become cracked and unsafe. They were either donated by parishioners or paid for with money raised by local fundraising. The bells were cast by John Taylor of Loughborough, and are operated by a lever mechanism located in the choir vestry and can be rung by one person.

Headley's Success at Leith Hill Musical Festival, April 1967: Four young Headley musicians won a trophy at this festival for their playing in the quartet competition.

The Headley Women's Institute in its 50th Year, 1968: This was a proud and well-deserved achievement, commemorated throughout that year by functions which referred to the time when the Institute was founded in 1918 and its development after that. In 1965, it produced an admirable 'Scrapbook on the History of Headley'.

Last Days of the Village School, March 1970: The Village School's closing down was particularly sad because it had carried on successfully for so long – since the 1860s. There had apparently been staffing problems for some years and since this continued to be difficult it was decided to close the school early in 1970. It is worth recalling the Headmaster's last brief entry in the School's Logbook for 25th March 1970: 'After a continued existence for 107 years this Village School finally closed today'. An assembly to mark the event was held at the school, with Colonel Bibby and the Rector (the Rev. Lloyd Jones) attending. After some presentations the school was dismissed for the last time.

It took some time for the Headley families to accustom themselves to having no school nearby. Most of the children went to attend the Poplar Road School in Leatherhead and a special bus was provided for their journey to the new school.

The old school building is now the office of the Surrey Association of Boys' Clubs.

Queen Elizabeth's Silver Jubilee, 7th June 1977: Headley celebrated this event in traditional style. Early in the day a Thanksgiving Service at St Mary's Church celebrated the 25 years of the Queen's reign. During the morning and for the rest of the day flags were flown in parts of the village.

'900 Years of Headley's History', 1985: This was a large and well supported fête designed to show in a practical way how Headley has

Fig. 28. Headley School, 1970. Staff and pupils on the day the School closed down, 25th March 1970.

developed since Norman times. There were talks and exhibitions on some of the events which may have affected the village, also references to some of the families who once lived here. The ancient sport of falconry was demonstrated with six birds of prey and wardens from the National Trust presented a display on the old ways of making fences. Hand-made lace was on show by an Oyster Hill lace-making group. Local wood carving was also there to be seen. Many side-shows and Morris Dancing added to the fun of the occasion.

Festival of Village Arts and Crafts, 1992: The Mole Valley District Council supported this festival which was a great success.

Headley Village Day, and the Flower Show: This has been a popular summer attraction for several years. More than 700 people attended in 1999 and about the same number were there in the Millennium Year.

Headley welcomes in the new Millennium Year: The Christmas

Fig. 29. Former School House, off Church Lane.

Fig. 30. Flower Festival at Headley Parish Church, 1983. *Courtesy, K. Scowen F.R.P.S.*

celebrations at Headley in 1999 were soon followed by the start of
the Millennium Year on 1st January 2000. On the evening before this
there was a service close to midnight at St Mary's Church, with the
bells ringing soon after the stroke of 12. A dinner was held in the
Village Hall, prepared by a leading chef, the Hall being lit by candles
and decorated with silver birch saplings. After midnight there was a
firework display as more than 100 Headley families danced along
Church Lane.

Headley Today

Despite the many changes in land use during the last twenty years,
Headley remains an unspoilt Downland village, with green fields,
woodlands, the open spaces of the Heath and splendid views of the
country all around from St Mary's Church and its spire. The continuing, essentially rural, aspect of Headley derives in part from the
fact that so much of the land is owned and managed by conservation
bodies like the National Trust, the Surrey Wildlife Trust and the
Preadland Estate. May this continue to be so for a long time.

Notes

Most of the information in this chapter is based on the following:
Headley Parish Records (SHC 6187/5/1–2) at the Surrey History
Centre, Woking
Headley Manor Court Book, 1834–1939: SHC 4416
Headley School Logbook: SHC CES/27
Headley WI Scrapbook (1965)
Agricultural Records by J.M. Stratton (1978)

The National Trust at Polesden Lacey, Surrey Wildlife Trust,
Headley Court Defence Services Medical Rehabilitation Centre and
Tyrells Wood Golf Club also provided much useful information.

Chapter 8

POPULATION

When the first Census was taken in 1801 Headley's population of 217 was in marked contrast to the neighbouring parishes of Ashtead and Leatherhead (populations of 552 and 1,078 respectively). This difference continued during the next two centuries when the latter parishes, unlike Headley, experienced a remarkable growth. By 1991 the population of Headley had grown to 709, that of Ashtead to 13,363 and that of Leatherhead to 9,746. The contrast between Headley and its neighbouring parishes has been well illustrated in an article by E.C. Willatts, some time ago, covering the period 1840-1932, which, though only dealing with Headley and Ashtead, reveals the difference in character between the three parishes.[1] This comparative approach has been taken as the basis for the present study of these parishes' respective populations at all periods.

Headley before the 1801 Census[2]

Whilst the starting point for modern population studies may be taken as the Census of 1801, and the accuracy of much early Census data may be open to question, various pointers exist to the relative significance of the three parishes, starting with the Domesday Survey of 1086. Such pointers, however, should only be seen as approximate indicators of the relative importance of the various settlements. Although it would appear that Headley, from the number of its villagers, was less than one third the size of Ashtead in 1086, it does not follow that this was reflected in the population figures.

The number of smallholders in 1086 at Ashtead was slightly over double that at Headley. The Lay Subsidy of 1332 gives a total of 18 taxpayers at Headley, which is smaller than both Ashtead and

TABLE 1: POPULATION SOURCES 1086–1801

	Headley	Ashtead	Leatherhead
Domesday Survey, 1086*			
Villagers	9 (100)	33 (367)	16 (178)*
Smallholders	5 (100)	11 (220)	12 (240)
Lay Subsidy, 1332			
Taxpayers	18 (100)	28 (156)	53 (294)
Communicants, 1603	100 (100)	120 (120)	260 (260)
Hearth Tax, 1664			
Houses	30 (100)	68 (267)	122 (407)
Hearths	62 (100)	172 (277)	300 (484)
*Estimated Population***	135 (100)	306 (267)	549 (407)
Compton Census, 1676			
Communicants	110 (100)	140 (127)	300 (273)
Bishops' Visitations			
Population, 1725	200 (100)	200 (100)	700 (350)
Population, 1788	200 (100)	150 (75)	919 (459)
First Census, 1801			
Population	217 (100)	552 (254)	1078 (497)

* The Domesday figures for Leatherhead relate to the combined manors of Pachenesham and Thorners.
** Assuming 4.5 persons per house (including children).
(Throughout this study, figures for Headley are adjusted to 100 for comparative purposes.)

Leatherhead, the latter being the largest of the three. This establishes a pattern which, from the available figures, appears to hold largely up to and including the first Census of 1801, and which is reflected in the data for much of the subsequent periods.

Three sources of data are available for the 17th century; the numbers of communicants in 1603 (see Table 1), the Hearth Tax of 1664 and the Compton Census of twelve years later (1676). These again show the same relationship between the three settlements, with the number of houses recorded by the Hearth Tax roughly doubling between Headley and Ashtead, and again between the latter and Leatherhead. Assuming an average of 4.5 persons (including children), this would give estimates of population of 135, 306 and 549 for Headley, Ashtead and Leatherhead respectively.

Population figures from the Bishops' Visitations of 1725 and 1788, and from the first Census of 1801, together with the estimated figures from the Hearth Tax, may be summarised as follows:

	Headley	Ashtead	Leatherhead
1664	135	306	549
1725	200	200	700
1788	200	150	919
1801	217	552	1,078

The same general relative pattern holds, but it is interesting to note that the Bishop's Visitation for 1725 shows Headley and Ashtead as having the same population. By the time of the later 'Visitation' in 1788 the population of Ashtead is shown as having dropped to three quarters of that of Headley. This seems strange in the light of Headley's location, off the main routeways, in contrast to Ashtead's position on a routeway between London and the South Coast. The veracity of the 'Visitation' figures may be open to some doubt. The fact that Headley is given a population of 200 in 1725 and in 1788 suggests that not all the figures cited in the latter year may have been revised.

Headley in the Census – the 19th century

By the close of the 18th century, the size of the populations of Headley, Ashtead and Leatherhead had established a relationship which can be recognised today. Throughout the period since the first Census, the population of Headley has been smaller than that of either of its two immediate neighbours but the difference is accentuated by a so far unexplained slump in the population of Headley, as is shown by the Census of 1821. Despite a decline in the population of Headley between 1851 and 1861, which was not redressed until 1891, its population almost doubled, from 217 in 1801 to 394 in 1901, an overall increase of 82%. This increase was, however, small compared with 241% at Ashtead and 335% at Leatherhead in the same period.

A snapshot of the local economy may be gleaned from the Census of 1831 (see Table 2). The prominence of agriculture at Headley, 35 out of 51 families chiefly employed, as compared with 60 out of 124 families at Ashtead and 81 out of 322 at Leatherhead, is immediately apparent. Five of Headley's farming families employed labourers whilst two were smallholders working on their own account. Altogether, forty labourers are reported as working in the village. There were very few retail and handicrafts at this time.

The Religious Census of 1851 shows that there was capacity (sittings) for about 140 people at Headley Parish Church and that on

TABLE 2: THE CENSUS OF 1831

	Headley	Ashtead	Leatherhead
AREA—Statute Acres	1,630 (100)	2,510 (154)	3,250 (199)
HOUSES—Inhabited	38 (100)	111 (292)	294 (774)
—Families	51 (100)	124 (243)	322 (631)
POPULATION	253 (100)	607 (240)	1,724 (681)
OCCUPATIONS			
Families chiefly employed in Agriculture	35 (100)	60 (171)	81 (231)
Families chiefly employed in Trade, Manufacture and Handicraft	4 (100)	20 (500)	136 (3,400)
All other families	12 (100)	44 (367)	105 (875)
AGRICULTURE			
Occupiers employing Labourers	5 (100)	5 (100)	2 (40)
Occupiers not employing Labourers	2 (100)	3 (150)	5 (250)
Labourers employed in Agriculture	40 (100)	93 (235)	137 (342)
Employed in Retail Trade, or in Handicraft, as Masters or Workmen	15 (100)	21 (140)	183 (1,220)
Capitalists, Bankers, Professional Men, etc.	3 (100)	6 (200)	53 (1,767)
Non-Agricultural Labourers	0 (—)	20 (—)	40 (—)
Male Servants	9 (100)	20 (222)	31 (344)
Female Servants	18 (100)	33 (183)	93 (517)

Sunday 30th March there was a total morning congregation of 118.[3] Corresponding figures for Ashtead are at least 380 sittings and a total congregation of 317, and for Leatherhead 580 and 550. These figures underline again the contrast between Headley and its neighbouring parishes.

Headley in the Census – the 20th century
Difficulties arise at Headley, as elsewhere, in examining Census data for the 20th century, due to cancellation of the Census of 1941 because of the war. The National Registration, although not directly comparable, may be taken as an indication of conditions at the out-break of the war, and the comparative figures for Headley, Ashtead and Leatherhead may be summarised as follows:

	Headley	Ashtead	Leatherhead
1901 Census	394	1,881	4,694
National Registration of 1939	*540*	*9,336*	*8,591*
1951 Census	591	9,852	8,562
1991 Census	709	13,363	9,746

These figures show increases of 37%, 396% and 83% for Headley, Ashtead and Leatherhead respectively between 1901 and 1939 and of 20%, 36% and 14% between 1951 and 1991 which must be taken as the limit of any post-war study. They should be seen in relation to the overall increases of 80%, 610% and 108% experienced between 1901 and 1991 (see Table 3).

TABLE 3: POPULATION OF HEADLEY COMPARED WITH ASHTEAD
AND LEATHERHEAD
1801–1991

	Headley		Ashtead		Leatherhead	
1801	217	(100)	552	(254)	1,078	(497)
1811	220	(100)	548	(252)	1,209	(550)
1821	184	(100)	579	(315)	1,478	(803)
1831	253	(100)	607	(240)	1,724	(681)
1841	317	(100)	618	(195)	1,740	(549)
1851	363	(100)	684	(188)	2,041	(562)
1861	322	(100)	729	(226)	2,079	(646)
1871	337	(100)	906	(269)	2,455	(728)
1881	339	(100)	926	(273)	3,533	(1,042)
1891	415	(100)	1,351	(326)	4,305	(1,037)
1901	394	(100)	1,881	(477)	4,694	(1,191)
1911	419	(100)	2,921	(697)	5,491	(1,310)
1921	521	(100)	3,226	(619)	5,817	(1,116)
1931	487	(100)	4,783	(982)	6,916	(1,420)
1939	*540*	*(100)*	*9,336*	*(1,729)*	*8,591*	*(1,591)*
1951	591	(100)	9,852	(1,667)	8,562	(1,449)
1961	725	(100)	12,109	(1,670)	9,215	(1,271)
1971	758	(100)	12,950	(1,708)	9,518	(1,257)
1981	670	(100)	12,805	(1,911)	9,918	(1,480)
1991	709	(100)	13,363	(1,885)	9,746	(1,375)

1. Revised data for 1921 and 1931, taking into account the Surrey County Review Order, 1933, has been used throughout this study.
2. Figures for 1939 are taken from the National Registration. If not directly comparable with the Census data they give some indication of conditions at the outbreak of war.
3. Census data throughout is reproduced with permission of the Controller of Her Majesty's Stationery Office. © Crown Copyright. Thanks are due to the Census Customer Services, National Statistics, for clarification of recent Census figures.

The overall growth of the three parishes during the years since 1901 underlines the difference in the character of Headley's population from that of its neighbours, having remained largely rural in character, in contrast to the massive suburban development elsewhere.

Notes

1. E.C. Willatts, 'Changes of land utilization in the South-West of the London Basin, 1840–1932', *Geog. Journal*, 1933, LXXXII, pp. 515–28
2. This section is based upon information kindly supplied by David Robinson of the Surrey History Centre; see also John Morris (ed.) *Domesday Book*, Surrey (1975), C.A.F. Meekings (ed.) 'Surrey Hearth Tax, 1664' SRS. XVII, 1940, B.L. Harleian MSS 595, Anne Whitmore (ed), *Compton Census* (1986). For a general discussion of pre-Census data see Alan A. Jackson (ed.) *Ashtead – A Village Transformed* (1977), pp. 164–6
3. David Robinson (ed.), 'The 1851 Religious Census, Surrey' SRS. XXXV, 1997

Chapter 9

OLD HOUSES, COTTAGES AND FARMS

Headley has a number of houses, cottages and farms of historical and archaeological interest, some listed by the Local Authority and others reported on by the Domestic Buildings Research Group (DBRG) for Surrey. It is an impressive collection for a small village. Many of the buildings referred to date, at least in part, from the 16th to the early 19th century though the character of some of them has been altered in more recent times. The buildings described in the following pages are arranged by road, street or lane, as shown on the map of Headley (see p. 52), starting with those in the north of the parish and ending at its southern tip.

Headley Road/Clay Lane

Headley Court: This handsome house, now occupied by the Defence Services Medical Rehabilitation Centre (see p. 65), was built by the Cunliffe family in 1898 near to the site of an old farmhouse. The mansion-like building could be taken to be much older than it is; some rooms inside have impressive Jacobean-style panelling, probably dating from the 18th or even the late 17th century. The house is surrounded by beautiful gardens.

The Old House: A private tree-lined drive off Clay Lane leads to this house which was probably built in the 17th century. It is timber-framed with brick infilling and has a plain tiled roof.

Tilley Lane

Headley Park (formerly *Headley House*): The original house here was built in about 1800, a deed of that year giving the right to a water supply from Nower Wood for the estate. It is not known who all the owners were during the first 90 years but it was the home of Felix Ladbroke towards the end of the century. He sold the estate in 1895 to Mr J. Newton Mappin of the London jewellers, Mappin and Webb. The new owner carried out major work including a new wing but a disastrous fire in December 1896 totally destroyed the house and the Housekeeper perished in the fire. The house was rebuilt and occupied until 1949 when it was sold to developers who split the property into five separate units, as it remains today.

Park Corner: This house, sometime known as Beeson's Cottage after the Head Gardener of the Headley Park estate, was probably built around 1800. It was then most likely to have been quite small, but later in the 19th century four extra rooms were added and the roof was retimbered and extended to allow for this. A further extension was made in the middle of the last century. The present owners, Mr and Mrs Hugh Fortescue, have lived in the house for over fifty years.

Hurst Lane

Hurst Farm: The farmhouse dates from the 16th century, with some later additions. It is timber-framed with brick infilling and a tiled roof. There is a fine early 19th century dovecote not far from the house.

Slough Lane/Tumber Street

Slough Farmhouse: The original building, one of the oldest in Headley, is a three-bay timber-framed hall house probably dating from the early 16th century. It has an open hall in the centre and the two ends each have a bedroom above them. The front of the house is partly encased in brick. At some later stage a new bay was added, giving another bedroom and a back kitchen beneath it.

Dove Cottage: Like Slough Farmhouse, Dove Cottage, rented and owned by the Denyer family for about 170 years, was probably built

Fig. 31. Park Corner, Tilley Lane. *Courtesy, Stephen Fortescue.*

Fig. 32. Dove Cottage, Tumber Street.

in the early 16th century. It was originally an open hall house, with a chimney added in the 17th century when the house was flint clad. A century later a new cottage with its own hearth was added and extended with a donkey house lean-to at the end.

The old cottage was built with two rooms downstairs – the hearth room where the open hearth had been built in the centre of the floor; and the service room which had one bedroom over it. The stair up is in the back corner of the service room and is probably in its original position. The inglenook hearth has flint sides, a seat on the right side and a niche beside it; on the left is a bread oven.

Leech Lane/Tot Hill

Vine Cottage was originally a medieval open hall house of three bays and two storeys built in a fold of Tot Hill. It is built sideways to the road which winds up the hill and faces west towards the earlier north-south track which passes on its winding way from Headley Common to Headley Church. The building is rectangular, brick-faced in parts, with some timber framing; the roof is gabled and tiled. The entrance is to one side of the central bay and leads straight into the hearth room which has a bricked floor. The hearth is within the south end bay facing the large central room. There is a staircase up to the bedrooms at either end of the cottage, indicative of its open hall character.

Tuffets, a little further up Tot Hill, is a Georgian brick cottage which was originally called 1–2 Evelyns' Cottages; the present name was given by a recent owner from the tuffets of grass which were in the garden. The cottage is set at right angles to Tot Hill, on a platform levelled out of the rising ground. It has two rooms on each floor and the staircase between them rises directly and steeply up to the bedrooms; there is a step up to each bedroom from the small square landing. The hearth room downstairs has an inglenook hearth.

The Old Cottage faces sideways to the road which turns at right angles just below it to descend Tot Hill. It was built as a medieval hall house, nearly hidden by modern additions, but the steeply pitched roof remains with an old outside chimney stack rising through a flat-tiled roof beyond. There is a lead drain-head to be seen dated 1743, though the main part of the cottage is probably as old as the early 16th century. Its entrance is into the back of the hearth room; carpenters' assembly marks are in the partition wall facing the hearth. The upstairs bedrooms have dormer windows.

Heather Cottage in a lane off Tot Hill, dates from the late 17th century when it was three cottages perhaps lived in by agricultural workers. One of the buildings is said to have been called 'Yeoman's Cottage', but a photograph of 120 years ago names the cottages as 'Rose', 'Lilace' and 'Heather'; the whole property was known as 'Heather Cottage' in 1945 (see Figure 9). The signature of the grandfather of the local builder, Stovell, has been found on one of the walls.

Heath House, nearby, is another old building with a handsome facade, probably built in the early or mid-19th century.

Crabtree Lane

Crabtree Cottage is in the lower part of this lane not far from Hyde Farm. It is an attractive old building in a fine position near Headley Heath and Lodge Bottom Road. The original cottage was probably built in the early to mid-18th century, its curved window heads being fashionable from about 1700 until 1750; window frames flush with the face of the wall are also consistent with an early 18th century date. It is, however, believed that some parts of the house may be older than this. The cottage is built of red brick with a slate roof. There are two rooms on each of the floors, with some later additions, including a loft. The front door and porch open into the living room with its large inglenook hearth. Exposed joists are characteristic of the period up to 1730 but their size suggests a later date. The cottage is shown on the 1840 Tithe Map when it was about a century or more old.

Church Lane

The Old Rectory, a short distance from this lane, suffered bomb damage in July 1944. After repairs it continued to be lived in by the Rector until the 1970s. It is now a private residence.

Webbs Farm The old whitewashed farmhouse dates from the 17th century; and Heath Farm, not far away, has some interesting old buildings.

Headley Common Road

Headley Hall (sometime known as **Headley Grove**). This impressive white stuccoed house, set in beautiful grounds, was probably built in its original form in the late 18th or early 19th century, though there are records of a much more modest building from as early as 1704 (see p. 33). It was then known as the 'Tiewood' estate but was being called 'Headley Grove' by 1809, about the time when the original house was likely to have been built. It continued as then erected for some 150 years, with a succession of owners, including the Ritchie and Ladbroke families in the mid-19th century, the Bordiers in the 1870s and Sir John Bridge, an eminent barrister and Chief Metropolitan Magistrate, in the later years of the century. The Maharajah of Baroda was the owner for a time, as was the famous racing motorist, Sir Malcolm Campbell. In

Fig. 33. Entrance Gate to Headley Hall.

Fig. 34.   Headley Hall.

the 1950s, parts of the original estate were converted into separate dwellings, but much of the house, apart from a few structural changes, was retained with its fine Doric columns and imposing portico. There are two lion heads in stone at the entrance gate.

Other Headley houses, though not 'old' in the context of this chapter, include **The Manor House,** off Church Lane, which carries a name well-known in Headley annals; it was for many years the home of Sir Ronald and Lady Wates. A short way south from here is **Great Hayes,** an impressive house near the Cricket Ground. On a lane off Tot Hill and close to the Heath is **Goodman's Furze** which has for a long time been the residence of the Bridges family. **Kingsbarn House,** near Tot Hill, is a fairly old property, restored and enlarged by Sir Michael and Lady Pickard. The late Stanley Pickard, father of Sir Michael, owned **Tumber House,** off Slough Lane, and its surrounding farm land. **Tunbarr House,** close to Leech Lane, was at one time called Oakdene Lodge; and its neighbour, **Tunbarr Cottage,** was once a bakery. For **Bellasis House** and for **Headley Court** see pp. 59, 65.

Notes

This chapter is based on information taken from Local Authority reports and those prepared by the Domestic Buildings Research Group (DBRG), Surrey. Hugh Fortescue's recent reprint of his articles in the Headley Parish Magazine have also been drawn on.

INDEX

compiled by J.C. Stuttard

Knyett, Lady Ann, 22

Ladbroke family, 33, 34, 40, 46, 82
Land sales & acquisitions (medieval), 18
Lay Subsidy (1332), 75, 76
Leatherhead, 1, 75–9; children from Headley
    attend school here, 71; St John's School
    Masters help Headley church (1905–06),
    53
Lee, Jane, 41
Legh family, 18
Le Homefield, 23
Leith Hill Musical Festival, 57, 71
Le Nore, 23
Lewis, Rev. J.F.O., Rector, 50
'Little Switzerland' valley, 6
Livery stables, 64
Livestock, 19, 24, 41, 42, 53, 63
Lloyd George's social reform, 53
Lloyd-Jones, Rev. B.R., Rector, 62, 71
Local Government Act (1894), 48
Lock, Tony, 67
Loretta Lodge, racing stable, 67
Lote family, 18
Lyall family, 41, 50
Lythgo, Sir William, Rector, 26

Manor House, 62, 63, 87
Mappin, J.N., 82
Massey, John, Rector, 27
Matthews, George, 47
Middle Ages, 17–21
Millennium Year (2000), Headley's
    celebrations, 74
Mole River, 4, 5
Montgomery-Campbell, H.C., Bishop of
    Guildford, 62
Moore, Arthur, 34; plans classical-style
    building, 31; William, 47
Morgan, Rev. Jonathan, Rector, 35
Motorway (M.25), 1, 65; Iron Age site close
    to, 12
Musters (1588), 29

Nason, Rev. John, Rector, 35
National Trust, 5, 64, 72, 74
Neolithic period, 11
Nettleford, Robert, 26
Nore, John ate, 18
Norestret, medieval road, 18
Norfolk, Duke of, 34
Norman Conquest, 17
North, Francis, Lord, 35
Norton, John, 'The Shires of England'
    (1595), 24
Nower Wood, geology of, 2, 4, 5, 7; spring
    from, 5, 38, 82

Nutshambles, field and early meeting-place,
    15

Observatories at Headley Rectory, 55
Ockle, William, 18
Old Cottage, 27, 84
Old House, 81
Old Houses, Cottages & Farms, 81–7
Old Rectory, 85
Open fields, 19, 23
Overseer of the Poor, 29
Oyster Hill, 1, 2, 5, 7, 57, 72; Spring at, 5;
    Forge close to, 47

Painters (1757 property), 37
Palmers (1809 property), 37
Parish Church of St. Mary, 20, 27, 35–6, 73
    (Fig.), 74; bells, 69–71; centenary
    celebrations (1955), 62; former church
    pulled down and new one erected
    (1850s), 42–3; in wartime, 59–61
Parish Council, 2. 48
Park Corner, 82, 83
Peasants' Revolt (1381), 20
Percivall, Andrew, 33
Phillips, Rev. J.E.R., Rector, & distinguished
    astronomer, 54, 55 (Figs)
Phillips, J.R., 42
Pickard, Sir Michael & Lady loan Headley
    Cricket picture, 87; Stanley, 87
Plescy (or Plecy), 17, 18
Poor House, built on the Waste (1753), 38
Population, 20, 25, 37, 49, 58, 75–80
Postal services, 47–8, 69
Potterscroft Field, 18
Pound, enclosure for animals, 37
Praed, Humphrey Mackworth, 7
Praedland Estate, 9, 74
Presbyterian 'Classical System' for Surrey
    sanctioned (1648), 28
Price, John, architect, 31
Pullen, William, 41

Reading Room, 49
Reindorp, George, Bishop of Guildford,
    dedicates new church bells (1966), 69–
    70
'Relief of Protestant Refugees in Ireland'
    (1642), 29
Restoration (1660), 29
Richbell, Philip, 35
Riders' Association, 67
Ritchie family, 34
Roads, 19, 20, 29, 48, 82; M.25, 65
Rocque, John, 1770 map, 37, 42, 48–49
Roman occupation, 12–15
Rowland, William, 37